LET ME KISS IT BETTER

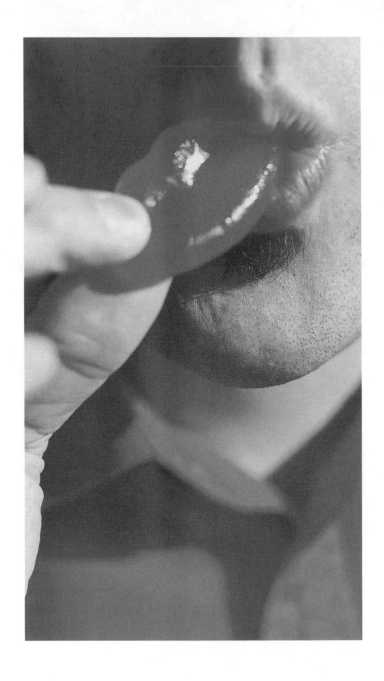

Billeh Nickerson

LET ME KISS IT BETTER

Elixirs for the
Not So
Straight and Narrow

ARSENAL
PULP PRESS
Vancouver

ARSENAL PULP PRESS
103-1014 Homer Street
Vancouver, B.C.
Canada V6B 2W9
arsenalpulp.com

The publisher gratefully acknowledges the support of the Canada
Council for the Arts and the British Columbia Arts Council for its
publishing program, and the Government of Canada through the Book
Publishing Industry Development Program for its publishing activities.

Book and cover design by Solo
Editing by Mary Schendlinger
Cover photograph by Rosalee Hiebert
Printed and bound in Canada

NATIONAL LIBRARY OF CANADA CATALOGUING IN PUBLICATION DATA:
Nickerson, Billeh, 1972-
   Let me kiss it better : elixirs for the not so straight and narrow/
Billeh Nickerson.

   ISBN 1-55152-125-3

   1. Gay men – Humor. 2. Canadian wit and humor (English)* I. Title.
PN6231.H57N52 2002   C818'.602   C2002-911148-X

For Matt Davy

Contents

9 Author's Note
11 Acknowledgments

ONE
15 The Seven Men Who've Cut My Hair
21 The Classic Dong
23 Smells Like Teen Spirit
25 Australian Hot Dogs
27 The Langley Lesbians Connection
29 Spermists
33 Garden of Earthly Delights
35 The Problem with Parrots
37 Wet Bar/Baby Change Table
41 Truth, Justice, and Gold Lamé
45 Heart-Shaped Pubes
47 My Very First Screwdriver
49 Games People Play
51 Bad Underwear
53 Drinking and Dialing
55 Gay Bag
57 Avon Calling

TWO

61 Red Hot Sonja

65 Wishbones

67 Hand Solo

71 Frequent Fucker Points

73 Bring Your Own Fag

75 Nice Cum Face

77 Dildo in the Dishwasher

79 Who Has Seen the Lesbians?

81 Cheese Day

83 Through the Microscope

85 Protein Whores

87 Incredible Hulk Kisses

89 Hung Gay

91 Dirty Dogs Only

93 The Old Up-Down

95 Big One in the Bathhouse

THREE

99 Let Me Kiss It Better

103 Scruples Optional

105 The Dry Hump Bandit

107 What's In a Name?

109 Snap Crackle Poppers

111 Up the . . . Nose?

113 Gaysicles

115 If I Had a Hammer

117 My Left Tit

119 Mr BC Leather 2000

121 Going Bananas

123 Come Prepared

125 Gayland

127 The Cock in Cocktail

129 The Moaner Sixty-Niner

Author's Note

During the writing of this book I came to understand how acceptable it was for perfect strangers to come up to me and tell me what they use to wash their sex toys: dishwashers, pots of boiling water, antibacterial cleansers – everything, including the kitchen sink. I'd stand there thinking, I don't know you but I know how you clean your dildos. It doesn't get much more personal than that. But who am I to be so shocked, since it was my article in a local paper or my performance at a cabaret that made them feel comfortable enough to come up and talk to me?

I suppose their behaviour is to be expected when I write and perform the things that I do. I'm sure people who write about plants get told stories about ferns and rose bushes all the time. It just so happens that I often write about sex, and sex between men, and what it's like to live in a world where not everyone else is sex positive. So instead of fern and rose bush anecdotes, I get to hear about cum towels and the things people stick up their bums. People tell me these stories at parties, supermarkets, movie lineups, bus stops, airport lounges – pretty much everywhere, and with each story I feel the line between the private and the public blur.

But not everyone appreciates my musings. One bathhouse owner pulled a publication in which I had speculated about what to do in a bathhouse in the event of an earthquake. Maybe if he took the time to use his own facilities he wouldn't be so uptight. Writing this book has also made me realize that you can't take anyone's support for granted.

As strange as it may seem, one of the biggest influences on this collection is *Sesame Street*. Much of my wild imagination, not to mention my love for vignettes, stems from the countless mornings of watching Big Bird and Kermit the Frog and all the *Sesame Street* inhabitants as they worked through yet another day. In that spirit I'd like to remind readers that this book was brought to you by the number 69 and the letters s and M.

Stay sexy,

Billeh Nickerson
Vancouver
September 6, 2002

Acknowledgements

Thank you to the following:

the fine folks at Arsenal Pulp Press for their
ongoing support;

my editor, Mary Schendlinger, one of the best
in the biz;

Gareth Kirkby, for giving me my first break and
keeping the sexphobes at bay;

Aislinn Hunter, Craig Moseley, Teresa McWhirter,
Michael V. Smith, Sheri-D Wilson; and
Rosalee Hiebert and Brad Cran for their
wonderful photographs.

Thank you also to those friends who listened to
earlier drafts of these works, and everyone who
shared (or had stolen) their secrets.

Some of these pieces first appeared in slightly
different form in *Faggo*, *Front* magazine and
Xtra! West. Thanks to the editors for supporting
my work.

ONE

THE SEVEN MEN
WHO'VE CUT MY HAIR

First Barber
Richmond, B.C., c. 1975

The first one I remember, who cut my hair when I was three, had white hair like Santa Claus and a blue uniform that I would later associate with dental hygienists and hospital workers. I remember hating the cape and having to hold still while my mother and grandma stood there all proud, or something close to proud, this being a significant event rather than an everyday occurrence like eating breakfast. I was small and felt even smaller because the chair, the booster seat, the barber's hands – everything, even the scissors – was so big. He never smiled, so I thought that I'd done something wrong. It didn't matter that they gave me a candy afterwards. I think I cried.

Stephano
Langley, B.C., c. 1979

Stephano told my mother that I was handsome

and should keep my hair longer around the sides. He wore a Dorothy Hamill-like wedge and pulled it back from his face to show her that his bone structure, like mine, required a frame. His salon was located in a strip mall complex that also included a bank, a deli, and a gift shop that sometimes sold Mexican jumping beans. Stephano wore tight pants and open-collared shirts that always seemed to match the blue salon walls, in the same way his rings and gold chains matched the gold trim on the mirrors and picture frames. Once he asked me if I played "close" with my cat, because he thought the rash on my scalp might be ringworm. How did he know that I had a cat? It scared me to imagine what else he knew.

Bryan
Langley, B.C., *c.* 1983

Bryan, who owned a single-seater barbershop in the middle of my hometown, has cut my hair more than anyone else, man or woman. No matter what we talked about, the conversation always came back to his truck. I don't recall ever seeing his truck, but to this day I dream of him driving around with his barber's scissors resting on the dashboard or passenger seat. And there was a time in my life when I wanted a truck like the one Bryan described to me. A big truck. Four tires, mud flaps, all sorts of big truck things. When I sat there with Bryan and all the other men in his shop, the war veterans, the motorcyclists, the three generations of men – grandpa, dad, and son – who had got kicked out of the house to go get haircuts while the women prepared special dinners, I felt I belonged, but then I'd go home and shower away the loose hairs and feel different again.

Bryan wore white or cream-coloured long-sleeved shirts, with small collars that exposed a patch of chest hair. Even when he lifted his arms or bent over to pick up the broom and dustpan, his tucked-in shirt never pulled out of his pants. This still amazes me, almost as much as the amount of hair that could accumulate on a busy summer day in the corner of his shop. I took pleasure in identifying which part of the hair mass had come from me, as if we were all building something together.

Trips to Bryan's offered me something else: a chance to watch my father interacting with men in semi-social settings that didn't include his friends or the old stubby beer bottles of my youth. I would sit watching my dad while Bryan talked about trucks, taxes, and politics, and I would see my father nod his head or stay still, a non-response that often signified disagreement. As well, with the exception of my grandpa, Bryan was the only man who ordered my father to do something ("Keep your chin up") and got obeyed. My father still mentions Bryan from time to time, whenever he talks about finances and *The Wealthy Barber*. "How do you think Bryan saved for his truck?" he muses. Whenever I encounter anything that is the same colour of blue as the disinfectant in the glass jars of combs that stood on his workstation counter, I think of Bryan. It still makes me feel manly.

Barber at Fantastic Sam's
Langley, B.C., c. 1987

In retrospect, I realize that the old man with the pierced ear who cut my hair at Fantastic Sam's wasn't a sailor, as I thought at the time, but a homosexual suffering the indignity of having to cut hair at a workstation with a stupid name like Happy or Bubbles spelled out on the mirror in front of his barber chair. This was the first man who had cut my hair since Bryan, and it felt strange. I had been getting my hair cut at Fantastic Sam's for a year, during which they had only employed women. Then they hired this man, and suddenly they became concerned about matching genders and all the male clients were put with him. We didn't talk much, but I could tell he wasn't happy. This was pre-AIDS, pre-gay-friendly suburbia. Did he think I was gay? Did he feel sad for me, as I feel sad for him now? Did he survive the plague? Did he have someone who loved him? I can't remember whether or not I liked his haircuts, though I do remember liking it when he stopped working there and the women started to cut my hair again, a memory that stings like a razor nick to the ear.

Luigi
Victoria, B.C., c. 1994

Luigi, the Italian, cut my hair while serenading me with selections from the opera. All the old men sitting around waiting would hum along or tap their canes while he sang. At first it didn't feel like getting a haircut, but like walking onto the set of a spaghetti commercial or walking onto the beach, for whenever Luigi pumped the barber's chair with his foot it seemed as if he was inflating an air mattress. My body tingled each time he pulled my ears back out of the way to get at stubborn hairs or to trim my sideburns. Sometimes I wished he would pull harder or grab my entire head and kiss me. He must have been sixty years old. I always feared he'd see my erection pushing up against the cape or notice how heavy my breathing had become.

Jamie
Victoria, B.C., 1997

Jamie came over to my apartment to cut my hair because I'd been summoned to a last-minute job interview. We'd broken up a few months earlier and I was embarrassed to have to call him under such circumstances. He stood behind me for a change, his kneecaps nudging my back as I sat on the floor in the middle of my living room. The occasional glimpse of the scissors moving around my head made me aware of how vulnerable I was. Every once in a while he blew the loose hairs from my neck, a gesture that would have been an intimate one only a few months earlier. When he held my face in his hands to tilt my head, I thought of all the times he had done that to kiss me from a different angle. I felt ashamed, for early on in our relationship I had shaved my head bald, not because I liked it better that way, but because I knew he'd hate it.

Tino
Vancouver, B.C., 2000

Tino still looked good in a tight shirt even though he was in his fifties. A friend had recommended him because Tino always brushed your head with a wire brush, and the sensation was akin to scratching your entire body all at once. Even though he held his scissors in an almost dainty manner, his demeanour was that of a hungry worker about to plunge a fork into a juicy steak. As he cut my hair I'd stare at the Dolly Parton poster and the Princess Diana postcard on his wall. He'd talk about the weather, the squeegee kids, the bald spot at the back of my head, and when he'd nod to me, it felt like machismo. Whenever I pass his shop, I want him to run his metal brush over my head again. I want to sit in his barbershop with every man I've ever waited for a haircut with. Every grandpa, every dad, every son. Every *Sports Illustrated*, every *Popular Mechanics*, every newspaper sports section. I want my big truck waiting outside for me. And I want my hair in the pile on his floor.

THE CLASSIC DONG

My dildo adventure started when a friend who I would never have guessed would purchase a dildo – or at least purchase a dildo then tell me about it – spoke of its many virtues. I think his exact words were, "It makes me cum like the dickens." I don't know exactly what "the dickens" means or where the expression came from. It makes me think of Charles Dickens and Oliver Twist or Ebenezer Scrooge, all decidedly unsexy things. But I could tell by my friend's face that "the dickens" was a good thing that I too needed to explore.

While touring the sex shops on Vancouver's Granville Street (it's important to comparison shop, even for dildos) I learned many things about myself. For instance, I found out that the word *jelly* does not excite me in the slightest. I also learned that I'm not the kind of person who is turned on by dildos shaped like the signs of the zodiac. I did, however, wonder briefly whether it is more exciting to use a dildo in the shape of one's own sign or of a compatible one. It would add a whole new dimension to the age-old pickup line, "What's your sign?" I silently thanked my parents for giving birth to an Aquarius, the water bearer, and not a Gemini, the twins. Ouch.

After many trips to many stores, I decided upon a basic model. The package called it a "classic dong." The sales clerk exclaimed that I had picked a good product and gave me washing instructions in the same way people in clothing stores give helpful hints about caring for the jeans you just bought. Apparently, dishwashing detergents with antibacterial agents are just as effective as expensive cleaners. I thanked the clerk and wondered whether I had just learned the real reason why that manicurist on the dishwashing detergent commercials thinks so highly of the product. I'm sure she soaks in it all the time.

Back at home I noticed a sticker that read: over one million sold. Had I become the kind of person who purchases something because of its popularity? Had I just bought the dildo equivalent of a Shania Twain CD? But I didn't want to make hasty judgements before I had tried it. The proof would be in the pudding. So to speak.

Later that night, before I tried it out, I found myself thinking about those one million dildos. That's a lot of dildos. I wondered how far they would stretch if laid end to end and I started converting inches to feet to miles and so on. It worked out that one million versions of my dildo would stretch out 203 kilometres. Enough to get from New York to Atlantic City with dildos to spare.

The next day my friend asked me how it had gone, and whether I thought my dildo smelled like Barbie. I told him it may have smelled like Barbie but it sure felt like Ken.

Smells Like Teen Spirit

One spring evening, I took a straight friend out to experience a night of gay Vancouver, and as we sat in a Davie Street restaurant, she asked me why it smelled like cum. I was relieved, for I thought I had been imagining things. Throughout the meal I had surreptitiously sniffed the waiter, my friend, the patrons from the other tables who happened to walk by – anyone and anything I could get my nose on. I even did a quick mental play-by-play of my day to make sure the smell wasn't emanating from my loins or my chest or the tops of my shoes.

Until she spoke up, I had felt like a truffle pig, but now my behaviour was justified. Why would we smell cum in a restaurant? There was no choice but to investigate further.

My friend speculated that the smell was coming from the dishwasher. I immediately had a vision of some sweaty, zitty teenager with bugged-out eyes, giving the best that he had to his chafed, forlorn penis. I then realized that my friend meant the machine, not the human dishwasher, and I was relieved. Dishwashing is hard enough, without the additional responsibility of scenting an entire restaurant for a whole evening. Kind of gives a new meaning to dishpan hands.

We never did identify the source, and I never thought about it again until sometime later, when I visited the same restaurant with a different friend, a lesbian. The restaurant smelled cummy, as it had before. After a few minutes of what I hoped was discreet snorting, I asked her if she smelled what I was smelling. Much to my shock, she did. Let's put it this way: when a lesbian thinks that something smells like cum, goddamn it, it really smells like cum.

What the hell is going on? Are they piping the scent out into the dining room with a huge fan, as bakeries are known to pump the smell of cinnamon out onto the street? Is this some capitalist ploy to attract the gay dollar by manipulating our noses? Are gay men that shallow and predictable? It would be one thing if they were selling new cars, because new cars sometimes smell like spunk, but they sell nachos. Spunk, nachos – I don't get the connection.

Is this like the practice of female French secret agents during World War II of dabbing vaginal juices behind their ears to lure German officers? I'll tell you a secret, guys. If I wanted to eat my dinner accompanied by the smell of man juice, I'd stay at home and eat Kraft Dinner with my cum towel wrapped around my shoulders. In other words, if you want to keep my business, get some essential oils or hang car deodorizers from the salt and pepper shakers. And get some fresh buns, too. Yours are always stale.

AUSTRALIAN HOT DOGS

The 2000 Olympic Games in Sydney, Australia, are just another blip in everyone's memory now. Kind of like Crocodile Dundee, or the *Love Boat* episode where the crew sails down under. But for me, an Olympics junkie, the games that year were a reason to go into therapy. I'm still trying to recover from those awful body suits that the Olympic swimmers wore, instead of the once ubiquitous Speedo.

Talk about the end of a tradition. I used to look forward to those Speedos even more than the opening ceremony with the lighting of the torch. For me the games don't really start until I've seen my first gentle giant cavorting around the pool in his nut-huggers. Forget the torch; it's Speedos that light my fire.

Sure, I love the personal success stories, the athletic prowess and the politics of judging, but nothing proves more dramatic than a tall man in a small Speedo. Talk about a situation ripe with tension. Where's the drama in a body suit? Half the fun of watching swimmers was waiting for someone's dick to pop out.

They shave practically every inch of their bodies, shave their eyebrows and sometimes their heads, but if one of them gets an erection – hello water drag, goodbye medal. Can you imagine training for a lifetime only to lose because part of you became a little too excited? Bad dick. Down dick, down. In high school English class I learned that Olympics contests should be thought of as Man vs. Man, or Man vs. himself. I have since learned to add a third category: Man vs. his cock (in women's events, woman vs. her breasts).

The most obvious body suit culprit has to be the Aussie swimmer Ian Thorpe, also known as the Thorpedo. Everyone knows that it's not the size of a torpedo that counts, but rather how you deploy it, but I can't stop thinking about him and about what could have been had he worn a Speedo. Thorpe swims around the pool propelling himself with his size seventeen feet. It doesn't take a rocket scientist, or a torpedo scientist for that matter, to figure out that seventeen is a magic number. If I've learned one thing from my Olympics-watching days it's the bigger the feet, the bigger the . . . endorsement contract.

Now that I think of it, why don't they just cancel the whole swimming competition and replace it with an event to see who can get their Speedos on the fastest? Or have four-man relays where the first swimmer has to put on and take off his Speedo, then pass it on to his teammate. The 4x nut-hugger. That way even countries without pools could compete, and the International Olympics Committee wouldn't have to worry about doping. Some drugs help you take your Speedo off faster; I can't think of any that would shorten the time it takes to put one on.

Long live the Speedo! May it continue to hug the world's best.

THE LANGLEY
LESBIANS CONNECTION

For as long as I can remember, Santa Claus (AKA my mother) has put a pair of nail clippers into every one of my family's stockings every Christmas. I never thought about this until a friend of mine lamented that she can't have long nails any more now that she's decided to sleep only with women. I didn't understand her at first. She told me to think about it. I did and now I believe that the Langley lesbians have been stealing my family's nail clippers for the last twenty years.

What else could it be? My mother bought four nail clippers (one each for Mom, Dad, my sister, and me) every year for twenty years, which means that eighty pairs have gone missing. It's not like they've been donated to a war effort scrap metal program, or melted down to make a bell for the community church, and no one close to my family makes sculptural art from domestic objects. Even if my cat had taken the nail clippers to get revenge for all the times we dulled his claws, we would have come across a few pairs in the garden or on the lawn by now.

I always felt a secret lesbian presence in Langley,

my old hometown, and even more so during the few years when k.d. lang lived there, but I had never suspected that they partook in undercover operations to liberate nail clippers from suburban homes. I'm not upset, though. Actually, I'm quite flattered. I'm just surprised that the lesbians have kept this nail clipper thing a secret. How come lesbians don't wear nail clippers around their necks, the same way Janet Jackson used to wear keys and rave kids used to wear little bottles of soapy water so they could blow bubbles? Why don't they just hook a pair of clippers onto the shoulder of a leather jacket in the same manner as men did with cock rings a few years back?

Maybe the Langley lesbians have kept the nail clipper business secret so that Madonna doesn't find out and exploit it in a video. Picture Madonna singing beneath a sickle-shaped object you think is a moon, until the video ends and you realize it's actually a giant nail clipping. Within a few short weeks, everyone and their dog would be wearing nail clippers. You would be able to buy them in assorted colours at chain clothing stores. Polka-dotted, leopard- and zebra-printed, neon and glow-in-the-dark. High-society women and news anchors who think themselves funky would pin them on their dresses and power suits.

I have to hand it to the Langley lesbians. They have already figured out how quickly nail clippers would turn from trendy to tacky in the mainstream world. So if you live in Langley, or any other city, and your nail clippers have gone missing, just forget about it. You've made some lesbian out there very, very happy, and you've helped prevent yet another embarrassing and expensive fashion disaster.

Spermists

My favourite T-shirt is navy blue with the word SPERM printed on the front in yellow letters. At first I thought it was one of those corporate rip-off shirts, in this case SPAM, but I soon realized that it had transcended T-shirtdom. It had become a mobile conversation piece, like one of those A Day in the Life of picture books, only on my chest instead of a coffee table.

Before I bought the shirt I rarely used the word *sperm*. It's not a word most people say every day. Even when I talked about reproduction I always avoided it. In one family management class in my high school, the teacher made the whole class say the word *penis* over and over until it no longer felt embarrassing. Maybe this is what I wanted to do to the word *sperm*.

I can tell a lot about people by the way they react when they first see me in my SPERM shirt. People who run away probably don't own Marilyn Manson records. Those who nod their heads in approval or laugh out loud probably don't vote for right-wing politicians. Men who give the thumbs-up sign as if the two of us were wearing identical sports team jerseys watch far too much televison sports.

Dozens of men have come up to me and started conversations about sperm and how it connects us, as one stranger put it, "all the way back to Adam and Eve, man." I can't wait for the day I come across a colony of men trekking out to a forest in matching SPERM shirts so they can play drums and rediscover their primal selves: New Wave Masculinists. Spermists.

It's not always fun to be wearing my SPERM shirt, though. For instance, one evening as I rode through Surrey – the big-haired head-banger capital of the world – on a SkyTrain full of men with tight jeans and hockey hair, I felt that my SPERM shirt had become a liability. Being the drama queen that I am, I held one hand up to cover my chest, only to realize that if I just hid the S, my shirt displayed a most Surrey-appropriate PERM.

Another time I was walking through a mall when I bumped into a couple of nuns. And as I hightailed it out of there, I stumbled upon a Brownie troop. The Brown Owl or Tawny Owl or whatever big bird Brownie leaders are named after gave me one of those looks that suggests you have single-handedly ruined the world. I felt like saying, "It's just sperm," but I was afraid I'd get jumped by some social do-gooder. Who knows, maybe one of those resourceful Brownies will turn her experience into a new brownie badge – an I-survived-going-to-the-mall-and-seeing-the-man-with-that-word-on-his-chest badge.

It's amazing the response a single-word on a T-shirt can provoke. I'm considering a whole new line with words like OVUM, CLIT, FORESKIN, MENSTRUATION, and PROSTATE. It will be interesting to see the response that each shirt gets. In the meantime, I will continue wearing my SPERM shirt with pride in hopes that people will finally realize we've all needed sperm at least once. Whether we like it or not, it's half the yin and yang of life.

GARDEN OF
EARTHLY DELIGHTS

One of my best friends heats vegetables in the microwave before sticking them up his ass. Carrots, zucchini, cucumber, you name it. His own personal little shepherd's pie. After he told me, and after the initial shock of visualizing a toasty eggplant shoved up his bum had worn off, I thanked him for sharing. That he had found a way to overcome the perils of cold carrots reaffirmed my belief that the gay community has some of the most creative and resourceful individuals in the world.

Once I knew this intimate fact, it came as no surprise that this friend, like almost every other politically progressive householder I know, has organic vegetables delivered right to his door. All this time, I thought people liked the produce service because they liked vegetables. In actuality, they were all celebrating the hand delivery of a custom cornucopia of organic sex toy possibilities.

The reason my friend and I were discussing sexual experiences with vegetables in the first place was because another friend had said she found it reasonable to whack off with a cucumber, then peel it and put it in a salad or use it for a facial. While others would consider a cucumber a disposable one night stand, this woman viewed it as a reusable gift from the gods. My toasty eggplant buddy was shocked. He would never reuse veggies, he'd only heat them up.

My cucumber friend went on to mention that she suspected her house sitter of whacking off with the vegetables, so she pulled them all out of the fridge to give them a good once-over in the sink. Why she would let someone she suspected of diddling with her carrots take care of all her worldly possessions was one thing, but that she would consider eating those same carrots was quite another. This from a woman who gets upset when people double-dip chips at parties.

For the record, I don't own a microwave, nor am I the kind of guy who sticks vegetables up my ass. But even if I did, I doubt that I would use them again in salads or cosmetic masks or even a celebratory post-coital cucumber sandwich. And if I suspected someone else of using my mini zucchini as a dildo, I'd throw it into the garbage so fast you'd hear the thud from miles away. If someone sticks a vegetable inside of their body, it should never be used again, not even as a garnish. Compost it if you want, save the seeds and make your own little garden of earthly delights, but under no circumstances should that carrot or cucumber or any other vegetable ever make a return trip to the refrigerator. And if you stick your veggie sex toy in the microwave, make sure you pop in a meat thermometer before using it. A few extra seconds of nuking can turn a toasty zuke into a red-hot poker.

The Problem with Parrots

J asper is a parrot and the beloved pet of Heather and Gillian, the lesbian couple who live upstairs, and he loves to mimic the sounds of telephones, neighbourhood cats and cheesy construction workers.

Every day without fail I hear him parrot the ringing phone and then say "Hello," as if he were answering it. Sometimes when I've just exited the shower, I'll hear his construction-worker style whistle; even though he doesn't intend it for me, it still makes me feel sexy.

I used to find Jasper amusing until it dawned on me that he is probably learning to repeat the noises emanating from my room. It would be okay if he said "Ooh baby" or "Oh yeah" or "Yes! Yes! Yes!" He could pick that up anywhere. Unfortunately, I'm convinced that the dialogue will be more gender-specific, such as "Suck that cock" or "Come on and lick those balls, big boy." You don't have to be a graduate of Lesbian 101 to figure out that dykes generally don't talk like that.

If Jasper is picking up sounds from my apartment, he must be picking up their noises too. But if he starts to scream, "Lick my clit," I'll just laugh. He isn't my parrot. Why should I care? What isn't funny is having someone else's parrot mimic your most intimate sounds. It's like teaching someone else's dog a trick it will only do for you. Never screw with someone else's dog. Karma will come and bite your ass one day. Big time.

I am now in what I call "cope mode," a mind-set where I constantly imagine the worst situation possible, in hopes that when something actually occurs it will be far less traumatic, and more a relief than a reason for therapy. In cope mode I visualize one of two situations.

The first occurs late in the evening, while Heather and Gillian host the annual Ms Dyke Commercial Drive in their living room. All the cool dykes are there as judges: Ellen, k.d. lang, Rosie. Just after they remind everyone of the important role of Ms Dyke Commercial Drive Runner-up, and just before they announce the winner, Jasper launches into a spate of "Show me your cock! Show me your cock! Show me your cock!"

The second unfolds early in the morning, just as I sit down for breakfast. I can hear Heather and Gillian making love in the bedroom above me. Just as I start into my grapefruit or yogurt or whatever people eat for breakfast these days, Jasper screams, "I love your balls, I love your balls, I love your balls!" I never eat breakfast again, and consequently, I become one of those grumpy people they warn you about in elementary school. Friends stop returning my calls, my cat moves in with the family down the street, I become addicted to the Internet, and I am never seen again.

So far, neither of these situations has come about and I can still be a potty-mouthed trash talker in bed – if I so choose. Either Jasper is a well-adjusted parrot or he's discreet. I hope he stays that way.

WET BAR/BABY
CHANGE TABLE

Anyone who has never had children has probably overlooked a whole category of interesting and economical home furnishings – baby apparatus. I purchased my very first baby change table at Value Village a few years ago, for fifteen dollars. At the time, I wondered if my womb envy had finally got the better of me. I've had fantasies about being the very first man to give birth. I've even considered donating my sperm to female friends who are fed up with straight men. But all that usually stops as soon as I think about my student loans or the price of daycare. How can I raise a child when I can't even afford a new pair of Fluevog shoes?

But I had to have the table. I just loved the way those baby blue teddy bears danced around with pink elephants and other after-dinner-mint-coloured animals along the puffy vinyl surface of the table. It was like a Benetton ad for a pastel animal world. United colours of plush. The minute I saw it in the store, I knew that it stood for all the things I hold sacred in my life: dancing, cultural diversity, kitsch, childhood memorabilia, and organized drinking.

Once I got it home, I stuck it in the corner, because that's where all the moms I've known over the years have put theirs. Then I stood back and looked at it, as if I were visiting an art gallery and trying to understand what one of the pieces "meant." After a while I went to my liquor cupboard and took out every single bottle. The table was a double-decker, so I put all the hard alcohol on the top shelf and all the wine bottles – the unopened ones as well as the empties to achieve a fuller effect – on the bottom shelf. The beer stayed in the fridge.

Whenever friends came over to my apartment, they would ask me why in the hell I had a baby change table. I would sit them down and pour them a drink before explaining the virtues of the baby change table/wet bar:

1. The table has four sturdy legs. No matter how messy you get, if you lean up against it, chances are you will still manage to pour the perfect drink. Believe me, I know.

2. The animal-character-printed puffy vinyl tabletop allows for easy wipe-ups – even those pesky red wine spills.

3. You can hang a bar towel in a convenient yet classy manner on the metal rod at the side.

4. If your model includes a baby bath, you have an ideal ice bucket.

5. You can have a little bondage fun with the plastic strap on the table, which is used to fasten your baby to the table so it doesn't roll off.

With the exception of my mother, who almost had a heart attack when I told her I had just bought a baby change table, everyone I know has enjoyed my wet bar. So the next time you walk the aisles of a furniture store searching for that perfect piece, don't overlook the baby department. You just might surprise yourself.

Truth, Justice, and Gold Lamé

Growing up in the suburbs of Vancouver on the edge of the Bible Belt, I learned the value of fantasy. While all the other neighbourhood boys drove their BMXs around the block pretending to be Evel Knievel, I spent hours and hours spinning around in circles, convinced that if I spun fast enough I would magically turn into Wonder Woman, or somehow summon Wonder Woman through a magical conduit. The result was always the same: I wound up in a dizzy heap trying not to puke on Dad's lawn again, but a still little voice pushed me to keep trying: "Spin fast enough and she will come."

There was method in my madness. Even at the young age of seven or eight I knew it would take someone as wonderful as Wonder Woman to make my hometown bearable. Instead of clichéd muscle-bound action heroes, who left me bored silly, Wonder Woman walked around saving the day in her high-heeled boots and bullet-proof bracelets – thus proving that you can be both powerful and accessorized at the same time. Instead of building ramps and flying over someone's little sister on my bike, I learned, as the theme song says, to "fight for my rights in my satin tights."

Maybe I was drawn to Wonder Woman, and to other metahuman heroines such as the Bionic Woman, Jeannie from *I Dream of Jeannie*, and Samantha of *Bewitched*, because no matter how hard they tried to fit in or what evils they saved the world from, they never seemed to be truly accepted. They could successfully fend off terrorists (as Wonder Woman did) and fembots (as the Bionic Woman did) or maintain a happy household (as Jeannie and Samantha did), but none could reveal her true identity of superhero, genie, or witch, so they were all excluded, which is the way I felt.

Although I didn't understand my gayness back then, I knew that I was different and would always be that way, no matter what. Perhaps watching Samantha or Jeannie clean the kitchen with the blink of an eye or the twitch of a nose affirmed the presence of an entirely different world, an underground culture that their neighbours wouldn't understand, but I did.

Now, twenty years later, I'm curious about how I resolved the contradiction between the "American Way" that Wonder Woman strove to protect and my own personal sense of right and wrong. While Wonder Woman battled Nazis and other threats, I fantasized battling all the rockers and their big-haired girlfriends who teased me at my elementary school and anyone who polluted the creeks near my home. Except for the few times I got angry enough to wish that Wonder Woman would attack my sister or parents, my fantasies seemed to match her missions: truth, justice, and gold lamé. Sometimes I still find myself wishing that Wonder Woman could save me – from evil student loan collectors, for example, or parking enforcement officers. So although networks cancelled her series a long time ago, don't be surprised if you see me spinning around in circles on a street near you.

Heart-Shaped Pubes

When my friend decided to drop her pants at last year's Christmas party and show everyone that her pubic hairs had been waxed into the shape of a heart, I realized just how rarely I get to see a cunt. I'm not talking younger-cousin cunt or foreign-film cunt, either. I'm talking live adult cunt. Heart-shaped pubes or not.

It's not like I want to see a cunt all the time. I mean, it wouldn't upset me if I had to see a cunt all the time, but it seems strange that I can count on one hand the real cunts I've seen in my entire life, including my mother's. Especially since I could fill a stadium with the number of cocks I've seen.

I told my friend about my dismal cunt-spotting record. She found my observation interesting but not profound, and said that sometimes she goes days without seeing her own cunt, let alone someone else's. "Cunts don't hang out like cocks do," she explained. Then she looked at me and asked, "Just where, exactly, did you expect to come in contact with cunts anyway?"

I thought about it but couldn't come up with any good examples. I'm not a flashy fashion designer who gallivants around naked models, I don't work in a strip bar, none of my friends like nude sunbathing,

I don't go to life drawing classes or work in a waxing parlour. Breasts I see quite often. Cunts, never.

At one time in my life, I saw a cunt almost every day. Paper ones, anyway. From 1979, the year I discovered my father's *Playboy* collection, to 1984, the year my family started to get *National Geographic*, I must have seen thousands of them. I spent most of the time with The Year in Sex and Sex in Cinema issues, since those were the ones that consistently showed naked men, but whatever you're searching for in a *Playboy*, you'll always come across a cunt.

Apart from the Suzanne Somers issue, where I saw Chrissy from *Three's Company* naked, I tended to ignore all the women, just as I carve around the chocolate and concentrate on the strawberry and vanilla in Neopolitan ice cream. Since seeing my friend in all her heart-shaped glory, I've realized that I don't need to taste the chocolate in order to appreciate it. Nor should I just ignore it. No matter the shape, it's good to have around.

My Very First Screwdriver

When the film crew that had been working in my apartment asked if they could dismantle my bed to make room for their video equipment, I told them I'd break it down myself. Had it been any other piece of furniture I would have made them do it, but beds are different.

I've often envisioned numerous men grunting and sweating around my bed, but those visions always include me. I didn't want men taking my bed apart, I wanted men in my bed. And if I couldn't have them in my bed I would take the bed apart myself. Even if I had to phone my father for help.

During our conversation I had to put down the phone a few times to run into the bedroom and study the details, and eventually I could report to my father that the screws holding my bed together had little square indentations, not slits or xs. My father said that I would need a red-handled Robertson screwdriver. I thanked him and set out for the hardware store.

The event was shaping up as another chapter in my home improvement education, which had started on the previous Christmas when I received my very first hammer. Now I would be getting my very first screwdriver. Was it possible that I'd soon be buying a tool belt, or a bunch of undershirts? Is this how it feels to be butch?

During my walk I somehow got the screwdriver name mixed up and kept practising "red-handled Robinson." I even made up a little song to the tune of Simon and Garfunkel's "Mrs Robinson": And here's to you, red-handled Robinson, Jesus loves you more than you will know. Once I reached the obscenely large and intimidating home improvement warehouse, it took me ten minutes to find the screwdrivers. I considered asking one of the numerous staff where to find the red-handled Robinsons, but by some miracle I didn't and was much relieved to be reminded that it was Robertson. Just so I could leave the place without making a complete fool of myself, I announced to the cashier, "This is my very first screwdriver," in the stupid way of people who need to share momentous occasions with strangers.

"Great," said the cashier. No chit-chat, no red ribbons to tie around my precious new tool, no announcement over the loudspeaker that "This man has just purchased his very first screwdriver." At first the lack of spectacle made me sad, but then I accepted that this is the way people treat you when you're a butch man holding a red-handled Robinson – I mean Robertson.

GAMES PEOPLE PLAY

I'm wondering if anyone but me has a special ritual for keeping track of people they've slept with. For instance, I used to count all my lovers with my fingers. This one Cameron, this one Sam. That lasted a year or so, and then I ran out, so I started to use my toes. Eventually I had to consider the implications, if that soap commercial about your 2,000 body parts is true. I was uncomfortable about the prospect of one day looking in the mirror at "Jean-Guy," the body part formerly known as "nose": I already felt like all of my former lovers occupied my body as if it were a condo development, so I stopped counting.

Now, when I do play those games, they seem to be more challenging. Not exactly the *New York Times* crossword, but harder none-the-less. For instance, when the whole Free Trade debacle unfolded in the early '90s, I realized I had experienced my own personal NAFTA by sleeping with a Canadian, an American, and a Mexican. And during the last Quebec referendum campaign and the subsequent Canadian unity debates, I tried to figure out whether I'd slept with a man from every province and territory. I can't help but feel that I would have aided the "yes" side had I slept with more separatists.

One of my favourite rituals involves the alphabet. Take a piece of paper and write the alphabet down the left-hand side of the page. If you've slept with an Aaron or an Annette or anyone whose name starts with an A, write it down. Then continue with B, and so forth. Bisexuals may want to write in two separate alphabets or use two different-coloured pens.

If you find that too many of your lovers share the same name (why does every second one seem to be named Chris?), or that they all start with the same letter, improvise a bit. Use nicknames (Honeybun for H) or occupations (judge for J) or descriptions (guy with the really big nose for G). And don't forget the golden rule: if you're named Quinton, Xavier, or Zelda, or any name that starts with a rarely used letter, always wear a name tag. You never know when someone might want to complete their list.

Bad Underwear

I have a recurring nightmare where I'm trapped inside a car wreck, and while I sit there waiting to be rescued by the jaws of life, I realize that I'm wearing bad underwear. Not just unfashionable underwear, but ugly, discoloured underwear with the elastic all stretched out of shape. The kind of underwear that will instantly attract viewers' attention when the TV news people film the paramedics hoisting me, almost naked, onto a metal gurney.

When I wake up at the hospital my mother asks me if I'm okay, and when I say yes, she says that if only I'd told her the truth last Christmas, instead of saying, "I have more than enough underwear, Mom," I wouldn't have embarrassed myself and my entire family in front of all those television viewers. At this point in the dream I am usually overcome with intense pain, though I'm never quite sure whether it's because of the injuries I sustained in the car wreck, or the realization that my mother will now send me underwear care packages at Christmas, on my birthday, and every national holiday until she dies.

Sometimes the dream includes gay friends sending get-well boxes of Joe Boxer and Tommy Hilfiger. Other times a whole slew of lesbians carrying Tupperware containers enters my room for a get-well potluck. Invariably one of them tells me that I should be happy to have had any underwear on at all, since the alternative would have been for the news crew to bit-map my naughty parts and they almost always mess it up a little so people can see your bum. Somehow this comforts me. We hug. I make a mental note to hang out with more lesbians.

Another version of this dream features an ex-lover of mine, who used to wear the exact same brand, style, colour, and size underwear as I did. He struts up to my hospital bed and on his face is the look he always got when we had just had sex and couldn't figure out whose underwear was whose.

After I recover from the shock of seeing him again after such a long time, I realize he must have seen me wearing that ugly underwear and thought it was an old pair of his. When I ask him if he's here because of the underwear, he asks me if I still have his copy of Madonna's *Sex* book. "No," I tell him, "I don't have your book, and, thank you very much, I'm feeling quite better now. Maybe if you weren't so goddamn selfish all the time we would still be together."

I'm trying to inject subtle changes to my dream through meditation and one-on-one talks with my subconscious. These involve an underwear model taking pity on me after seeing my segment on the news, and making a spontaneous visit to my hospital bed to give me the underwear off his backside. So far it has yet to work.

Drinking and Dialing

Since I don't own a car, the closest I get to drinking and driving is drinking and dialing. That's when I come home from a night of painting the town pink and suddenly find myself lying on my bed with the phone in my hand. Although I am liable to D&D at any time of the year, I find it happens most often during the winter holidays. Some people spread their Christmas cheer with baked goods or crafts. I spread my Christmas cheer through late-night phone calls to friends in distant time zones.

It hasn't gotten to the point where I need a drinking and driving counterattack officer to Breathalyze me before I pick up the phone, but it has crossed my mind. "Officer, I've only had two highballs. Please let me phone Japan." Luckily I still have one built-in control: I live in Vancouver, and if you're an insomniac or a drinker and dialer living out west, you can't make late-night phone calls to your friends in eastern Canada. People in Toronto or Montreal can call you up after they leave the bar because it's not indecently late. If you live in Newfoundland you can get trashed, stagger home from the bar, and call your friend in Vancouver, four time zones away, and he'll still be watching

David Letterman. But for Westerners, it's overseas or nothing.

Consequently, Craig, my good friend living in Japan, has probably heard more of my drunken epiphanies than I'd care to count. And he gets to hear them uttered with the small-town twang that always accompanies even the most urban urbanite when D&Ding. When I'm drinking and dialing I lapse into the vernacular of the rocker kids who used to party around my hometown 7-Eleven. Every second word gets modified by "man"or "fucking." "Man, you fucking know I fucking love you, man." I'm sure Craig does.

I'm also sure that Craig knows a little bit too much about my sex life and the cocks of the men I sleep with. Maybe it's a writer thing, but when I D&D, similes such as "like a plum," "like a veggie dog," "like a big banana," or "like a fat baby's arm" tend to pop into my conversation.

My holiday drinking and dialing activity should not be confused with booty calls – when you call someone up with the specific intention of getting some late-night sex. In fact, phone sex when you're drunk can't even be called sex. With all that slurring, it ends up feeling more like a first-year foreign language course than an erotic session. Drinking and dialing gives you pleasure not from body contact, but from the simple knowledge that someone you love is listening.

GAY BAG

"I'm waking up straight tomorrow," I told myself. I took all my gay porno mags, videos, books, and anything that seemed too faggy, and put them in a bag. Then I put the bag inside another bag and then another, as if I were trying to wrap a gift for someone who always guesses what you got him before Christmas morning. After I had wrapped my gay bag, I put it under my arm and went out for a long walk.

Should I deposit my gay bag in one of those foul-smelling restaurant dumpsters in which TV detectives find bodies, or an obscure garbage can in a public park or sports field? It couldn't be just anywhere. And it definitely couldn't be where anyone would see me. I had to walk for a long time before I felt certain no one would be able to trace my gay bag back to me. I dumped my gay bag in a church parking lot. The garbage can was blue.

When I returned home from my walk I took a long, hot shower. I remember thinking I was just like those women in the hair dye commercial who sang, "I'm going to wash that grey right out of my hair," only it was gayness, and not greyness, that I hoped I could feel trickling off my body and down the drain.

That was almost ten years ago. I can't remember how many "I'm waking up straight tomorrow" days I've had. There must have been dozens. And I'm not sure whether to admire my own gumption or curse my shame. It's not as if those days made me straight – none of them worked for longer than half a week.

Recently I visited my parents' cabin in the B.C. interior. I rowed the rowboat, seadooed, watched loons dive and resurface, and walked around our cabin, shocked at all the knick-knacks my mother had salvaged from my childhood. Until then I had almost forgotten that part of myself.

For some reason, my mother's collection of decoy ducks, folk art carvings, and the various paintings and prints that once filled the walls of my childhood home made me think back to the days I thought I could de-gay myself by jettisoning everything gay from my life. Many of these things gave me pleasure. But a few items, like the photograph of the barn that once hung above the television set in the family room, made me feel as if I had just seen a ghost, the ghost of my former self.

Maybe that photograph reminded me of the excitement and the dirtiness I felt while watching male strippers on *Donahue* and *Sally Jesse Raphael*, or naked men on PBS or the French channel, or maybe it was just the shock of seeing something I had once lived with day after day for most of my life. Maybe that photograph made me confront my younger self and my early vulnerabilities. After that trip to the cabin, when I returned home to an apartment filled with all my gay things, I took comfort knowing just how far I'd come and that my gay bag days were over.

Avon Calling

The first time I made myself cum was with the plug-in foot massager my mother purchased from our neighbourhood Avon lady. I can't recall which Avon lady brought the massager into my home and became the catalyst – it was either the elderly woman who freaked out whenever I took my hamster out of its cage, or the younger, replacement Avon lady who always referred to her husband as "the husband" and whose husband always called her "the wife" – but I do remember that I was thirteen, that the massager was Kermit-the-Frog green, and that when I came I thought I would die, right there on the carpet.

The French refer to the orgasm as *un petit mort*, "a little death." While this may be an apt description, it didn't comfort my thirteen-year-old self. Whether it's a little death or a super jumbo death, death is death to thirteen-year-olds. Especially when you're covered in a mysterious substance. If only *Sesame Street* had prepared me for such a moment, instead of teaching me how to say "water" in Spanish, I wouldn't have spent the next few days believing that I was slowly deflating like a balloon. I still feel let down by Big Bird and all his friends. I have yet to use the word *agua* in conversation.

At that point in my life I'd only heard about cum. I'd never seen it, not even in a movie or magazine. I'd used it as a verb, an action, but never experienced it as a noun. The cartoon sperm that squiggled their way across the television screen during sex education class looked nothing like the stuff that covered my hands, arms, and torso, not to mention the green foot massager. I thought sperm would look like a bunch of little tadpoles, not a cousin to the blob. For a few days cum became the scariest noun around. It wasn't until the second time I used the trusty foot massager that I found out cum could also signify pleasure.

Besides wet dreams (which don't count, okay) this was my first cum, and whenever I think of it I experience a rekindled appreciation for Avon. I miss Avon. I miss the various toiletries that littered my family bathroom. I miss my father's musky soap-on-a-ropes and my sister's girly perfumes. I miss the festive soaps shaped like snowmen and angels and even Valentine's Day hearts, which always made me feel cleaner than ordinary soaps. I miss Avon calling.

Though it's been many years since that foot massager vibrated its last vibe on one of its two speeds – good and really good – I want to thank Avon for making such a sturdy, reliable product. And I want to thank the two Avon ladies who served my neighbourhood so well. Whether they knew it or not, they rocked my world.

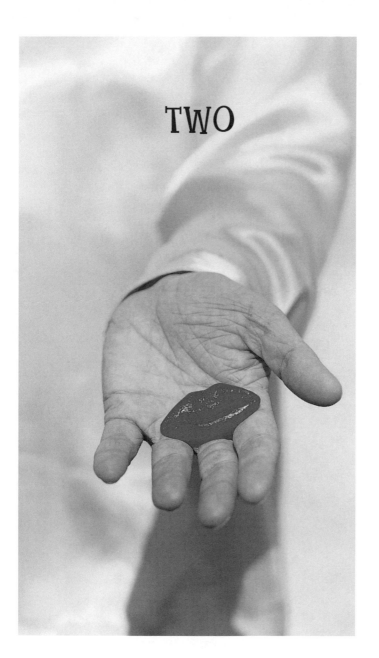

TWO

RED HOT SONJA

During the drive from the Student Union pub to the Red Lion, an infamous strip bar in Victoria, I wondered what the hell I was doing. I had never seen a female stripper before and it seemed strange to start now, at age twenty-five. I couldn't blame it on a few too many beers because I was sober; my friends were the drunk ones. I told myself that this was an adventure, a quest. That it was perfectly reasonable to have piled into a large pickup loaded with my fellow students, perfectly reasonable to have joined this trek to Nymphomania Week at the Red Lion.

The guys driving with me had a propensity to drink Jack Daniels straight, listen to Tom Waits, and throw glasses off rooftops whenever their relationships ended. I cared for them in the same way I care for all wild boys, and though I didn't try to sleep with them, I teased them in a way that was almost intimate. It was always about cock, never pussy, so by the time we reached the Red Lion parking lot, I was confused: why had my friends invited me out to see naked women, and why had I said yes?

The club reminded me of my hometown. Wooden interiors spruced up with hundreds of small Christmas lights. Framed mirrors painted with logos of once-popular beers. Men who wore baseball caps, white T-shirts, and denim. Denim, denim, denim. There was also a stage that reminded me of the cheesy fashion shows that used to go on at Willowbrook, a mall in my hometown. Unlike Willowbrook, the stage at the Red Lion had poles and a shower stall, and the performers there wouldn't be accompanied by the smells of the Body Shop and the sound of elevator music. But like the stage at Willowbrook, this one was brown and looked like it could fall apart at any moment. It made me crave Orange Julius.

Up on stage a woman with long, braided hair extensions danced around while men in the front row – my friends call it gynecology row – gawked at her crotch as if it were the only thing on stage, a magical dancing vagina. I ordered a dark rum and Coke from the cocktail waitress. She was frumpy and big-boned and when I realized I was comparing her to the stripper, I tried to think about something else, but I just kept staring at her until the stripper grabbed my attention with an upside down, legs-spread twirling manoeuvre on the pole.

I had only been with a woman once, on a dark beach with my boyfriend. It just happened. All that wine and the three of us, naked. I remember how warm her vagina felt on my face. How this surprised me. How my boyfriend wanted me to experience her because I hadn't, and I should. I couldn't really see how she looked, because the moon wasn't bright enough. I remember she felt warm. The warmth is most of what I remember.

Up on stage, the braided-hair stripper swayed her head seductively and it occurred to me that she looked like she was perpetually stuck halfway through a beaded curtain. When she did the splits and pushed her pelvis forward, one of the guys said, "Everyone loves pussy. It's where we all come from." I just smiled like someone who had nothing to add to the conversation. All the other guys clinked their drinks together in a toast to pussies. I ordered another.

As the braided stripper continued her act, some of the guys leaned forward to hide their erections. I knew that feeling, and I understood their pleasure, but not the source of it. When I was young I tried to excite myself with the *Playboys* my father kept under the stairs, wondering whether next month's playmate would do the trick.

When the stripper left the stage, my friends asked me what I thought of her. I said, "It didn't do anything, she didn't do anything for me. It was like eating rice cakes." Overhead, a loudspeaker urged us to get ready for all six feet of Red Hot Sonja. The guys in gynecology row began slapping the stage as if it were a giant communal bongo. My friends leaned forward again, this time in anticipation.

Red Hot Sonja came out on stage in big fuck-me boots like Julia Roberts' in *Pretty Woman*, only white vinyl, not black. She was so tall that her hair almost brushed up against the stage lights. She wore a pink negligee and a faux-pearl choker. I liked this woman. She was cheeky and sassy and walked around like a cruise director with attitude. I wondered if she'd had a boob job and for the next few minutes my friends and I speculated on whether her breasts bounced right, sat right, whether they were real or fake. Finally one of the guys said, "Shut the fuck up, like you're the boob expert," in the same tone my uncles used whenever I interrupted their baseball telecasts.

Red Hot Sonja had shaved her pubes. I'm told guys like it better that way, otherwise they'd be staring at hairy triangles. Guys like to see the goods. And, apparently, smell them – every time she sat down in front and spread her legs, men went right up to her crotch and took a whiff. They could get away with it, too: it was only against the law to touch the strippers. There was no law against paper-thin distances.

By the end of the night I had seen so much pussy that even sitting in a cramped truck full of men felt comfortable, not because of the close proximity of my friends, but because of my yearning for the familiar. I felt like a different man. Different from my friends and different from the man I had been before I entered the Red Lion, though I can't pinpoint why. As we drove past the turnoff to the beach where I'd had my first and only sexual experience with a woman, I thought about Red Hot Sonja and the braided-hair stripper. I thought of the men in the club and the men seated around me in the truck. I thought about all the women I've loved, and that night down at the beach, how I wanted to do a great job, how I really wanted to satisfy her, show her how much I cared.

WISHBONES

Apparently, the secret to sucking your own cock isn't the length of your cock, it's the length and suppleness of your neck. When I read this in Stan Persky's book *Buddies*, I didn't know whether I should thank him or curse him. Part of me now looks forward to starting a new and rewarding project – neck exercises – while another part regrets having wasted twenty years' worth of wishes: the times I blew out all the candles on my birthday cake, the wishing wells, shooting stars, public fountains – even the wishbones from the Thanksgiving turkey.

The first time it occurred to me that men could suck their own cocks was when I saw the Acrobats of Canton on ABC's *Wide World of Sports*. A woman faced forward with her chin flat on the floor and the rest of her body flipped over her, so that her feet rested on the floor on either side of her head, pointing forward. She also balanced piles of teacups, saucers, and glass bottles, but that part of the routine didn't interest me. I knew that if I had a body as flexible as hers I would be doing something other than balancing fine china.

I spent the next few years trying to become more flexible. Gymnastics, figure skating, impromptu ballet lessons on the staircase banister. (If you've ever wondered why so many gay men partake in such activities, wonder no more.) After many unsuccessful attempts, it seemed that fate was not on my side. Even with my new-found limberness, I still couldn't reach myself. Was it possible that only women like that Chinese acrobat could suck their own cocks? Had nature played yet another cruel trick?

Before long I had evidence that men, too, could perform such a feat. On an episode of the TV show *That's Incredible*, the three co-hosts blabbed on about the incredible flexibility of their guest, a male contortionist, while he squeezed into an incredibly small box. Afterwards the studio audience all screamed "That's incredible!" because he fit. I screamed "That's incredible!" from my rec room because he could reach.

Unfortunately, with even this role model I have failed in my quest. Believe me, I have never stopped trying or wishing. I still hope that each new day will be the one on which I crack open the fortune cookie that reads: "You will reach your cock today." Sometimes I have tried to enlist the forces of the universe, such as the moon's gravitational pull. But that was then. Now that I have read Persky and learned the secret to sucking my own cock, I'll just practise yoga and study giraffes more closely. I seem to recall something about extended space travel causing astronauts' spinal cords to stretch; i.e., their necks get longer, so maybe I will do some research through NASA. Has there ever been a gay in space? Where there's a will there's a way, I hope. Meanwhile, I keep wishing.

Hand Solo

Maybe this has happened to you: you go home with someone and when he excuses himself to go to the washroom, you walk around his apartment – only to realize that it's filled with *Star Wars* paraphernalia. Instead of photos of his friends and family, you are surrounded by Darth Vader, miniature storm troopers, and Yoda fridge magnets. The Force is with him.

When he comes back into the living room you still find him attractive, though you hope he doesn't have matching *Star Wars* bedsheets and pillowcases. You wonder whether he likes to assume different character roles in bed, and if so, which ones. You start to practise your Darth Vader heavy breathing. Suddenly, you remember c-3PO. What if he likes to pretend he is c-3PO? How do you make love to a rusty mannequin?

I've never been a big *Star Wars* fan. Even as a child I found the whole craze bothersome. I could never muster any pleasure in seeing my friends – the same friends who'd go around asking if I wanted some Hawaiian Punch, then punch me in the stomach when I said yes – carrying around big plastic tubes, AKA light sabres. I knew that boys would be boys, and that I would most likely be the first light sabre casualty. And the second. And the third. I knew early on that I would never be a Jedi Knight no matter how many times I practised with the cardboard cylinders left over from Christmas wrapping paper.

Now whenever I think of *Star Wars* I think of Mel Brooks' spoof *Spaceballs* – the Princess Leia-inspired character with the sticky, gooey cinnamon buns at the sides of her head and the Jabba the Hutt rip-off, Pizza-the-Hut, a creature oozing with cheese and pepperoni.

I hate *Star Wars*. Many of my gay friends fantasize about Luke Skywalker or Han Solo, or about being dominated by Darth Vader. I just shake my head. Forget top or bottom. If I'm looking for a partner, I will have to start by asking whether he likes *Star Wars* or not. It's one way of looking at the world.

I've often wondered just why it is that so many gay men love the movie and *Star Wars* culture. Here are a few possibilities: Darth Vader's head looks like a giant cock; "Han Solo" sounds like "Hand Solo"; Chewbacca is a nudist.

And even though the Ewoks appeared mostly in *Return of of the Jedi*, I thought about how they are early descendants of Shih Tzus and miniature terriers, both notorious as gay men's dogs. My theory is that long ago there was an intergalactic crash involving small dogs. When their owners weren't there to pamper them, the dogs learned to be industrious and resourceful. They worked their way up through the ranks until they became rebellious arms traders, not to mention highly skilled hairdressers.

Thank God my one-nighter didn't own a Shih

Tzu. It was difficult enough keeping a hard-on amongst all that paraphernalia, let alone a real-life Ewok whimpering for affection. And thank God that while my one-nighter may have believed in the Force, he also used the lube.

FREQUENT FUCKER POINTS

During a recent visit to Womyn's Ware to purchase a dildo for my friend for her birthday, I found out that buying dildos isn't like buying CDs. Sure, we had talked about dills and vibes before, but that didn't make me an expert on what my friend would want to stick inside herself. It's one thing to recommend lipsticks; it's quite another to recommend what to stick between lips. No matter how good my intentions – getting my friend off – I would have to cross the invisible line between well-wisher and personal space invader.

A wave of anxiety washed over me as I stood around in an ocean of shapes, lengths, widths, colours, batteries, and lubes. Dildo diversity at its best, but for me the selection only complicated matters. What if the dildo clashed with the colour of her bedspread? Or couch? You don't have to be Martha Stewart to understand how one small dildo can change the colour dynamics of a room. And if it wasn't a question of shape or colour, there were issues of practicality. For instance, I'd heard about an excellent dildo with an extension cord that plugs into the car lighter so that you can go at it while driving. I think I'll take the long way home. The perfect gift – only my friend doesn't own a car.

The pressure was unbearable. At least if you pick a bad CD your friend can return it or sell it used. You can't do that with dildos. I was determined that my birthday gift would not end up as yet another inappropriate sex toy left for dead in a dumpster or dresser drawer.

Finally the sales assistant recommended a gift certificate to avoid embarrassment or displeasure. That made perfect sense to me and I went right to the cash till. As we talked about the kind of men who enter the store – cool heterosexuals who understand the importance of satisfying their partners, and gays who understand that "strong enough for a man but made for a woman" applies to more than just deodorant – I pulled out my credit card as I would for any other purchase. Then it hit me like a slap: I would receive frequent flyer points for my friend's pleasure.

That got me thinking. Every birthday dildo, every condom, every bathhouse visit, every porno mag and drink bought in a bar with my credit card would get me frequent fucker points.

Now I have visions of myself sitting on a 747 en route to Europe, a cocktail in each hand, and my seatmate complaining about how much his airline ticket cost. I just look at him and smile. Poor guy – he obviously didn't get off enough.

Bring Your Own Fag

W hen a friend invited me to his house party and I asked whether any fags would be attending, he said, "No, Billeh, it's BYOF" – bring your own fag. Why had I asked? Had I become the kind of gay person who can only have fun with other gay people? Was I so dependent on gayness that I would soon purchase a pair of rainbow pajamas? Or sell all my worldly possessions, except for my Madonna CDs, and travel the gay party circuit for a year?

But no. I was just horny and tired of being ignored by cute straight boys. If I knew before the party started that I would be the only fag in the place, I could channel all of my energies into moderating thoughtful and evocative blow job discussions in the kitchen. If I knew that other fags would be attending, I would channel my blow job energies somewhere else.

I began playing the moderator role a few years back, when I decided to stop dancing to music unless it inspired me. While other party-goers strutted their stuff in the living room, I stood in front of the veggie plates discussing blow job techniques with women I hardly knew. It wasn't even a conscious decision. It just happened.

"Teeth bad, tongue good." "You don't have to suck all the cocks, just the ones you want to keep."

It's not like I'm an expert. I'm a man who gives blow jobs. Sometimes memorable, sometimes just a blow job. But for some reason women feel comfortable talking with me. This makes sense, because if I ever wanted to start eating pussy (like if something fell out of a building and landed on my head), I would beeline straight for my lesbian friends, especially the ones who put on a James Bond theme party called Never Enough Muff. I keep telling my straight male friends that if they started befriending lesbians instead of trying to seduce them, they'd learn invaluable secrets. But boys will be boys.

And women will be women. I'd be lying if I said I hadn't picked up a trick or two over the veggie plate. By the time we've eaten the carrots, celery, zucchini sticks, and all of the other phallic veggies, by the time we're left with too little dip and too much broccoli and cauliflower, we've written our own blow job Kama Sutra.

PS: I'd like to send out a big thank you to the woman who recommended sucking on a peppermint at the same time. It works. And although I now refer to you as that "woman who recommended sucking on a peppermint," I think of you often. And, in their own little way, so do my partners.

Nice Cum Face

A friend of mine has a knack for spotting people's cum faces. We'll be out for a walk or sitting in a restaurant when he'll grab me by the arm, point at someone and say, "I just saw his cum face." Police officers, street people, waitresses and university professors have all unknowingly revealed their most intimate facial expressions to us.

It's likely that he is seeing these people's possible cum faces, not their real ones, but it still catches me off-guard every time. The very act of pointing someone out makes me imagine that person having sex. If I agree with my friend, it means that I too visualized him or her achieving orgasm. If I disagree, then I still had to visualize someone's orgasm. There's no escape.

Sometimes my friend draws attention to my own cum face. This always puts in me an awkward position because I immediately become obsessed with finding out exactly what facial expression he saw. Invariably, I spend the next minutes trying to continue our conversation, while as discreetly as possible recalling how my face felt when he said it. It's hard enough keeping track of what my mouth says, let alone what my face does.

One time I was so disconcerted I excused myself

and went to the washroom to stare at myself in the mirror. I went through all the facial expressions I could remember wearing. It felt like one of those ridiculous warm-up exercises that drama teachers make people do. Yet I didn't see anything that resembled what I thought my cum face looked like. The one that came closest made me look as if I were trying to remove peanut butter from my teeth.

Maybe if I knew what my cum face actually looked like, I wouldn't end up in such a quagmire of speculation. What if someone hid a video camera and taped me having an orgasm? That would be unfortunate, but at least I'd have an unmediated view – the real McCoy. It's quite different to watch yourself in the mirror, or perform for someone when you know you're being videotaped.

Whenever I've seen myself cum, my porn star alter ego has kicked in. This is true of all men. Who wants to look like a complete dork at such a sweet moment? I think Robin Williams said it best when he described men at the point of climax as looking like Goofy, from the Disney cartoons. I agree; however, I have come across a few – or did they come across me? – who looked like Ethel Merman.

In any case, I've learned just to accept my friend's cum face talent. I just hope he keeps pointing out more cute coat check boys and fewer politicians.

DILDO IN THE DISHWASHER

J ust when you think you know someone, he tells you he cleans his dildos in the dishwasher. This is not one of those random tidbits of interesting information, such as the many times he has travelled to Portugal, or the fact that his grandmother was an Olympic athlete. No, your friend's admission about the dills in the dishwasher is downright shocking.

For one thing, it adds a whole new dimension to all those supper parties he hosted. I wouldn't call myself a prude, but every bowl, plate, knife, fork, and spoon suddenly glistens with potential dildo contact. Did he wash his dildos separately or with the dishes? How did he place them inside? Did he tuck them in those furrows meant for cups and glasses? Did he lay them flat where the plates go? Or did he stick them straight up in the cutlery containers?

Then again, if you have to use an appliance to sanitize your sex toys, the dishwasher is probably your best bet. Electric toothbrushes are abrasive. Washing machines may leave your dildos clean but the thump-thump of them bouncing around may leave you with a long-term hearing impairment. And although it may be effective to tie your dildo to the side mirror on your car and drive it through a car wash, it seems far too labour-intensive.

When someone tells me something that makes me question the sanity (or sanitation) of the habitants of our fine country, I tend to think about it for a while before taking a firm stand. This tends to bring out neuroses. What if the dishwasher door jams while washing your dildos and you have to phone up the lonely Maytag repairman? What if a visiting relative decides to help out by unloading the dishwasher, but mistakes the dildos for salad servers and brings them out at dinner to dish up her famous Caesar salad? "What lovely spoons, darling. You must have got them at Chintz."

To find out whether dishwashing dildos was recommended for dildos, I called my favourite dildo sellers at Womyn's Ware.

"This may sound like a stupid question, but have you ever heard of people washing their dildos in the dishwasher?"

"Only if they're silicone. And we recommend washing them without anything that has sharp edges. So don't put them in with the knives."

We also talked about how latex dills probably couldn't stand the heat. So make sure they stay out of the kitchen.

Not only have I learned that many people clean their dildos in the dishwasher, I have learned that I am the kind of person who will call a store to ask about it. In Boy Scout badges, that's the one with the dildo and the telephone. To all those people who wash their dildos in the dishwasher, thank you for being hygienic. You are not alone. Just keep the dishes separate, okay?

Who Has Seen
the Lesbians?

No matter how many times I move house, I always try to live on Commercial Drive, a funky but low-rent area on the east side of Vancouver, because I am a lover of cheap produce and cool lesbians. Never do I want to suffer the forty-five minute/two-dollar tomato syndrome. That's when gay men spend forty-five minutes getting their look together so they can drive ten minutes – two minutes driving and eight minutes parking – to a trendy supermarket to pick up a two-dollar tomato. I once heard an investor say that if you put all the money you would have spent on lottery tickets into an RRSP, it would be like winning the jackpot by the time you retired. The same must be true of the two-dollar tomato.

So the produce part of my vow has worked out quite well, but the lesbian part seems threatened. It used to be that even the softest whisper of "Melissa Etheridge" could start a riot on Commercial Drive. Somebody bring me some water. It could get hot and happening down here. Not even a World Cup soccer match between Italy and Brazil could generate as much excitement. Maybe I'm exaggerating a bit, but The Drive has definitely lost some of its dyke contingent. Where have all the lesbians gone? Or as the Quebecois squeegee kids say, "Où sont les lesbiens?"

It's not that all lesbians have left The Drive. It's just that the demographics seem to have shifted: for every two lesbians I used to see, I now see only one. Some people I talk to are not alarmed; however, if Sonny and Cher had been lesbians living on The Drive when they broke up, these people would have noticed the difference. I'm beginning to feel a void.

Lesbians keep me in check. Instead of asking, "What would Jesus do?" whenever I'm sad or confused, I ask myself, "What would a dyke do?" If I'm feeling a little bit butch that day, I say, "What in the hell would a butch do?" And if I'm feeling a little bit femme, I wear clothes that sparkle. If everyone, gay or straight, took the time to discover their inner lesbian, the world would be a much more harmonious place.

Anyway, if a massive dyke exodus is taking place from The Drive to suburbia or to the Gulf Islands or to some super secret magical dyke land, I hope the departing lesbians have a going-away Lesbian bocce tournament (bocce is like lawn bowling, only in the dirt). Lesbians vs. all the elderly Italian men in the neighbourhood and lesbians vs the Portuguese, and the much anticipated butch vs femmes. There could be a giant potluck and a bunch of East Van boys would put together cheerleading routines: Gimme an L, gimme an E, gimme an S, gimme a B, gimme an I, gimme an A, gimme an N. What's that spell? Lesbian! Lesbian! Lesbian! It sounds like a fun party, but I'd still prefer to see the lesbians at home, here with me.

CHEESE DAY

Today I tried to cross the street in front of my local park. I do this almost every day. Sometimes the drivers obey the crosswalk sign. Sometimes they even drive the posted speed limit of 30 km/h. Today they did neither. I stood there while car after car drove past me. Had it been any other day it wouldn't have been a big deal, but today was Cheese Day, the day I walk down to my favourite deli and buy my cheese supply for the week.

Just when the traffic opened up and it seemed that I'd be able to cross the street and continue my cheese quest, a brown car sped past me at sixty clicks. I flipped him the bird. It so happens I cut my nails this morning, so it wasn't an everyday kind of bird: this bird had class. I'm talking a Pierre Trudeau bird, full middle finger.

A few seconds after my beautiful bird took flight, I heard a loud screech and the ding-dong ding-dong of an opened car door. Then a forty-something bespectacled Italian-Canadian man started screaming, "You queer bastard, you queer bastard!" in the same clichéd voice TV actors use when they portray Italians speaking about love, pasta, or politics. I knew it had nothing to do with love or pasta, so I figured it must be my walking that was political.

At this point I didn't know whether he knew I was gay or whether he thought calling me "queer" would threaten my masculinity, thereby insulting my honour. I've been called "homo," "faggot," and "fudge packer" before, but never "queer." People are always telling me how progressive and all-encompassing "queer" sounds. Now I know that it depends on whose mouth it comes out of.

I didn't feel particularly gay when I woke up this morning. I mean, I feel gay all the time, but it's not like I wear head-to-toe rainbow beads or pink triangles. I wasn't even walking a small dog. Then I saw the look. The look rockers at my high school gave me whenever I passed them on the street.

I used to walk past them with my head down, or change direction, or just run past them. But today, when the man screamed, "You queer bastard!" I looked right into his eyes and screamed back at him about the right of way, and about how he should be ashamed, and then I kept walking. I heard a door slam behind me and then a loud screech as he drove off to wherever forty-something bespectacled Italian-Canadian men who yell "queer bastard" go to in such moments. I hoped that if he ran into those high school rockers, he'd tell them how much I've changed.

Through the Microscope

Unless one of my lesbian friends arrives at my apartment with a gold-plated turkey baster, I'm pretty sure my cum won't function as anything more than celebratory ooze. There are times, however, when I become aware that it could be used to make babies. This tends to make my cum seem different. It smells different. It looks different. It even feels heavier. And it has nothing to do with a change in diet or not drinking enough water.

I am reminded of a short film I saw at a gay film festival a few years ago, in which a character talks about how gay men leave their cum at rest stops throughout the country, but when they are asked to donate that same cum to make babies, it becomes as valuable as gold. Though I don't subscribe to any theories of cum alchemy, I do find the change in context makes my cum a different substance, a substance heavy with a new kind of potential.

Two recent events have caused me to think about this potential again: the first being my friend Carellin's pregnancy, and the second being a friend's experiment with a microscope.

For a while everyone just had to make a joke about me being the father of Carellin's unborn child. I confess we've sat on the same couch together and I've eaten her guacamole (not enough garlic), but for the record I am not the father of Carellin's baby. Still, even though I knew they were all joking, it felt strange even to consider, however briefly, that I might father a child after so many years of preparing myself to be the world's best uncle.

The second event was a friend's experiment: he decided to check out his sperm under a microscope. Being a resourceful fag, he didn't panic when he couldn't find any slides to use; he just took apart a CD case and spunked all over it. When he put it under the microscope – lo and behold! He saw his very own sperm sperming around like a bunch of speed freaks at an after-hours.

We were eating at a rib house when my friend told me his story, and for the rest of the meal, I tried to block out the conversations of the butch men around us while I visualized his sperm dancing around on that CD case, which had formerly housed Lionel Richie or some other unwanted music. It all made me want to cum on a CD case too, only my CD would definitely be one of Madonna's.

For some reason my sperm count has became important to me. It fills me with the same urgent curiosity that I feel when I walk past the Strong Man at the carnival and wonder whether my sledgehammer swing can ring the bell at the top. Though I've often ridiculed the man's tiger-print costume and physical prowess, I have always wondered how my own swing would fare in comparison. Since fathering a child seems like a high price to pay to satisfy a curiosity, it looks like I have a date with a microscope and a Madonna CD. And if that carnival Strong Man wants to come too, all the better.

PROTEIN WHORES

Everyone's a whore of some kind. Clothes whore, restaurant whore, selling-it-on-the-street whore, something. I'm a dollar-store whore. Sometimes I'll wake up and find myself roaming a dollar store with a basket filled with random items like bags of paper coin-rollers and happy face erasers. Another spatula? Why not. Cheap candles? You can't have too many.

For the most part, I embrace everyone's whorishness. About the only kind of whore that bothers me is the protein shake whore. You know the guys I'm talking about. The "I can't eat any of my own birthday cake because of the icing" kind of guy. The guy who falls in love with someone based on that person's ability to make fruit smoothies. "I've been with a lot of guys, but none of them made shakes like him. His shakes are so smooth even without banana. It was love at first sip."

I suppose it's better than dating someone because of his great hair or his cool shoes. Call me judgmental, but shouldn't love be deeper than the bottom of a smoothie glass?

And there's another thing: protein shake whores may look good – no, they may be so beautiful that you salivate at the very sight of them – but with every pro there is a con. And some cons smell worse than others. Let me say it bluntly: men who drink protein shakes fart all the time. I'm not talking the occasional thip-thip; I'm talking grandpa-after-Thanksgiving dinner, full-on tuba farts. And if you get a whole bunch of those guys sitting together in one room, it's like listening to a high school brass band in a sweaty gymnasium. Frankly, my idea of a good time doesn't involve protein shakes, a video, and numerous soundtrack additions courtesy of my partner's ass. Please, never let the words "Honey, was that you or the movie?" enter my vocabulary.

When I first embraced the gay community, I thought I'd left the farty boys behind. No more straight-boy roommates having fart duels in the living room. No more *Hockey Night in Canada* beer farts. No more let's pull out the lighters and see who can make a flame. I'm not suggesting gay people don't pass wind; I just didn't think it would be such a high-profile activity.

And what about the ozone layer? We hear about car emissions and cows with their four stomachs all the time; what effect do all those farting faggots have? It may be only a matter of time before Vancouver finds a lavender-coloured hole in the ozone layer above our city. Maybe the regional district should assess a levy for every protein powder container purchased instead of every car driven.

In the meantime, I will keep taking my oxygen mask to parties attended by protein shake whores, and hope that protein powder never becomes available in dollar stores. That could get messy.

Incredible Hulk Kisses

The scariest part of going to the dentist when I was a youngster was the possibility of getting an erection and not being able to hide it. You haven't felt truly vulnerable until you've pitched a tent while almost upside down on one of those motorized dentist chairs. The combination of having my hunky dentist's crotch inches from my eyes and having things pushed into my mouth by his hands inevitably led to unwanted boners in my rugby pants. The prick of the dentist's needle was nothing compared to the pain my own prick inflicted. To this day shame tastes like butterscotch fluoride.

The second scariest thing had to be the poster pinned to the ceiling that read: You don't have to floss all your teeth, just the ones you want to keep. How could my neurotic adolescent mind picture anything but doom? The message scared me then and it scares me now. My adult self remembered that poster when I read that brushing and flossing teeth before sex increased the risk of HIV transmission. Flossing wasn't limited to teeth any more; now it was about all of me.

Once upon a time, when I invited someone back to my place after the bar, I always discreetly excused myself at some point to the washroom, where I could give myself a quick wipe-down and brush my teeth. I'd go back into the living room with clean nether regions and breath that smelled miraculously of mint (and whatever liquor I had consumed that night). All that has changed. I still excuse myself for a few personal moments, but now when I find myself reaching for the toothbrush, warning bells sound inside my head: tiny cuts and abrasions! My toothbrush is no longer a dainty little accessory. It is a tool of sabotage.

I probably could have solved my predicament by using strong breath mints, but unfortunately I've never liked the stuff. I started using Clorets instead. Before long it got to the point where I'd bring Clorets to every place I could possibly have a sexual tryst, which means everywhere. I soon became the homosexual equivalent of Pavlov's dog: instead of salivating every time I heard a bell, I'd pop a Cloret whenever I sensed sex potential. To make a long story short, I chewed a fuck of a lot of gum and that gum made my tongue green.

At first it bothered me when my lovers asked about my green tongue. I'd act coy and meek. Then, one night during a stoned haze, I learned that my green tongue was not merely a frenzied Clorets-stained appendage; it was a miniature incarnation of the Incredible Hulk. It bit and chewed and slid itself inside the other guy's mouth with the bravado and prowess of an angry green man with ripped blue jeans and bad hair. I can't remember what the other guy felt, but that was one of the best kissing sessions of my life.

HUNG GAY

E very morning on my way to work, I take the
SkyTrain past Hung Gay Enterprises. At first
I just chuckled at the white trucks with *Hung
Gay* painted on the sides in large, easy-to-read
letters, but now, seeing them has become a ritual.
Some people drink coffee in the morning. Others
stand in front of the mirror and tell themselves how
good they are and how much people love them. I
only perk up after I've passed Hung Gay.

It's gotten to the point where if I turn my head
and miss seeing it, my whole day goes askew. I feel
empty and incomplete, kind of like that Cyndi Lauper
song, "There's a Hole in My Heart (That Goes All the
Way to China)." One morning a passenger stood up
and blocked my view, and I got off the train and rode
back a stop so I wouldn't miss seeing the trucks.

Hung Gay has become a personal mantra for
me. It transcends visions of eastern European studs
with cocks so huge you need to set an extra place
at the dinner table. It's more than Jeff Stryker. More
than that well-endowed skate boy you stumbled
upon one night. Hung Gay takes you to the upper
echelons of your being. And further.

I'm not sure what the other SkyTrain passengers
think about Hung Gay. Or about my humming. It

was a natural progression: every time I saw Hung Gay I'd say "Hung Gay" in a little whisper. Gradually it got louder, and now I just point my head into the direction of those trucks and hum "Hunnnnnnng Gayyyyyyyyy. Hunnnnnnng Gayyyyyyyyyy." Well, what would you rather hear between SkyTrain stops: "The next station is . . . Main Street/Science World" or someone humming "Hung Gay"? I can't think of a more beautiful sound. I've even noticed a few other guys enjoying it with me.

The last time a name had such emotional resonance for me, I was nine or ten years old and had just seen Lola Falana on the *Merv Griffin Show*. I remember saying "Lola Falana" over and over until I felt as if I had disappeared. But not even Lola can compete with Hung Gay.

When I started to write a column for a gay and lesbian newspaper, I considered doing some investigative journalism. You know, finding Hung Gay Enterprises in the phone book, and calling to ask what kind of business it was. I found the name in the white pages and was about to call when a little voice inside me screamed, "No! Why ruin a good thing?"

It doesn't matter what Hung Gay really does, whether it exports or imports, or deals in foodstuffs or furniture. In fact, the plain facts would destroy the beauty. I'd just like to thank Hung Gay Enterprises for having their trucks moving around my fine city spreading such an important message, and parking along the SkyTrain route to get me going early in the morning.

Dirty Dogs Only

Why do so many gay men bring their dogs to the park when they go cruising? I asked myself this question after someone's dog interrupted quite a hot session. We were having a "gay ol' time" when all of a sudden the man's dog started to bark and jump around us, snapping menacingly. Nothing kills a blow job faster than thinking Cujo has found you semi-naked and vulnerable in a forest. The dog acted like he was going to eat my dick for an appetizer and the rest of me for lunch. As it turned out, he had heard his owner moaning and just wanted to make sure everything was kosher.

Such is park sex in an age where people take their dogs everywhere. It's gotten so bad that it wouldn't surprise me to see the park littered with stainless steel doggie troughs like the ones they put outside Starbucks. Something's askew when men wearing leashes outnumber the dogs wearing leashes. Remember the good old days when people only brought kleenex, condoms, and lube? I'm one step away from adding doggie biscuits to my park party-packs. Anything to placate those pesky canine tag-alongs.

I like dogs. I'm just tired of watching a parade

of Benjis and Lassies and Rin Tin Tins sniff about my feet while I'm doing the nasty. And I can't help feeling that the dogs are comparing my techniques to all the others before me. Performance anxiety is bad enough, but verges on the unbearable when coupled with the critical looks of a know-it-all canine. If I could talk to the animals, I'm sure dogs would ask me why we don't get splashed with a garden hose like they do.

Guys, if you need to share sexually intimate moments with your dog, then smear your body with peanut butter and keep it out of the park. My idea of foreplay does not involve throwing a big stick every few minutes so I can make out with someone in the time it takes the dog to go and retrieve it. Felch boy, I mean fetch boy, fetch!

If it were a St Bernard with a portable wet bar strapped to his body or a Lassie-wannabe that magically appeared whenever you ran out of lube, then I could deal. Making out with someone while he tries to persuade his dog to play dead, just isn't sexy. It's not fair to the dog and it's not fair to me.

For all those guys who think they can fool people into believing that they're just walking their dog and not looking for sex, I have one thing to say: everyone knows that people who walk that far into the bushes aren't on some nature hike, unless they have bongos. If you want to fool people you need a better disguise. Try dressing up as a tree or a squirrel. Or, better yet, why don't you just come as yourself?

THE OLD UP-DOWN

So I was walking down the street, minding my own business, not cruising too much, just doing my own thing, when this cute guy walked by and gave me the old up-down. At first I was tempted just to ignore him, since I find the up-down thing lame and unoriginal, but something about his up-down made me turn around. After placing one hand strategically to the side of my crotch and feeling with my thumb to ascertain whether my fly was properly zipped (it was), I turned around and gave him a little up-down of my own.

It turns out I knew the guy from somewhere. Only I couldn't remember where from. Each of us gave the other one of those "I know that you know me" casual wave/head nods and we both kept walking, so I was left in the wake of a very irritating mystery. I spent the better part of that day dusting my brain to dig out where and when that cute guy had left his prints on my memory. I didn't know him from high school, college, or university. Not from the bus, SkyTrain, or any other form of public transportation. Not a gay club and not a straight club. Not the corner store or my neighbourhood bank. Not funky vintage clothing shops and definitely not the Gap.

After ransacking my mind to dig up all the places I usually recognize people from, I narrowed my list down to three possibilities: I had either a) slept with him, b) made him a latte, or c) slept with him and made him a latte. I kept telling myself that this sort of thing happens to everyone. It's the late nineties. People have numerous lovers. They serve numerous customers. Sometimes they get confused. Blow jobs, lattes, the edges become blurry. But when I described the incident to a bunch of my friends, all of them looked at me in a way that made me wonder whether the word *slut* was written across my forehead.

By this time I was sorry I had stopped for a second look at the guy. The floodgates had opened and I didn't know if my brain could handle all the images of people who have ordered lattes, cappuccinos, and espressos from me, at the same time as all the images of people I've slept with. Believe me, it wasn't pretty. I still haven't solved the mystery, but I do know this: the next time someone gives me the old up-down, I'm just going to keep on walking.

Big One in the Bathhouse

When you live on the West Coast, there are three things you can't escape: death, taxes, and media reports about when the big earthquake will hit. They tell us it could be tomorrow, it could be today, it could be three hundred years away, but we should always be prepared. Such reports always include helpful hints, like the fact that toilets and canned vegetables are an excellent source of water during emergencies. This may be useful, but what I want to know is: What happens if the big one hits when I'm in a bathhouse?

Will I just keep doing whatever I'm doing, because I assume that all the shaking is from the guy in the next room taking it extra hard? Will I be trampled to death by a mob of panicky white-towelled men? Will I miss the whole thing and then compliment the guy for having such a deep throat? Will someone have to inform me politely that the glory hole I'm enjoying is actually a crack in the wall caused by the earthquake? All of these thoughts ran through my mind as I sat through the Health and Safety Committee meeting at work.

Usually such meetings cause me to think about having a highly visible and fully stocked first aid kit.

My mind wanders to fire safety or band-aids that don't hurt when pulled away from your skin. But at one recent meeting, I found myself wondering where I could take cover in a bathhouse during an earthquake. No desks. No tables. Nothing whatsoever that could be considered shelter. It's pretty slim pickings, boys. Not counting the ubiquitous white towels and the other bathhouse patrons, I couldn't think of a single item to hide under.

In real buildings I know that it is best to rush to the nearest desk or doorway, but the walls in between bathhouse rooms offer as much support as a fifty-year-old bra. Have you ever watched a house of cards collapse? It may be more advisable to cover your body with lube so that when the roof caves in, it will just slide off you.

On the other hand, while a well-lubricated body may protect you from the structural damage, it won't save you from an even more horrific fate: a bathhouse full of men simultaneously dropping their poppers. If the smell doesn't get to you, the disappointment will.

About the only bonus to being in a bathhouse during an earthquake would be the improved odds of finding a date. "I'm not sure if we'll live through this, but if we do, can I have your phone number? In the meantime, keep sucking!"

I suppose there would be another bonus reserved for those patrons of a bathhouse located one floor above a Subway restaurant. If the floor gives way and you fall into the Subway below, I doubt that they'd deny you a sandwich. It probably wouldn't be the type of twelve-incher you were hoping for, but hey, beggars can't be choosers.

THREE

LET ME KISS IT BETTER

Maybe I suffered too many skinned knees when I was a child, but to this day, I still associate kissing with making things better. I kiss the heads of crying babies and meowing cats, the casts of friends with broken arms – I've even found myself kissing inanimate objects like wonky televisions or finicky computers.

The first person I kissed was Valerie Davies. I kissed her knee. She was probably ten, maybe eleven. I must have been eight. It was a big deal. I remember kneeling down as if to propose, but I kissed the scab on her knee instead. From that moment until I was in my early twenties I didn't kiss anyone romantically. Sure, I kissed family members, drunks under the mistletoe, and exchange students from Quebec – one kiss for each cheek – but none of those counted. In retrospect, I'm not sure how that happened. I wasn't some religious fanatic trying to save my purity. In one moment my lips were pressed against Valerie Davies' knee, and in what felt like the next I was sixteen and had never been kissed. Then seventeen, then eighteen, then nineteen, then twenty, then twenty-one, then twenty-two.

A few months after my twenty-second birthday, I met a boy who wouldn't kiss me until I had kissed him first. We'd met on classics night at some straight bar that doesn't exist any more. Our first song was "Life in a Northern Town." He wore a red turtleneck and we dirty-danced through that song up until the end of Barry Manilow's "Copacabana." I wrote down his number on a bus transfer, and when I called him the next afternoon, we agreed to go out on a date. I bought us a bottle of white wine, which we drank out on a boat dock, under the stars. I felt terrified, nauseated even. All these details seemed to come part and parcel with the kiss: the club and its music, the red turtleneck, the bus transfer, the white wine, the dock, the stars; my lips pressed against these things as much as him. Never has the space through which I bent down to reach another's mouth ever seemed as long a distance to travel.

The strange thing about my sex life since that time is that more often than not, kissing has not even been first base. It's as if I always have to run past the pitcher and head for second or run the wrong way to third, or just spin around in circles on home plate. Am I impatient? Am I afraid of intimacy? Are my partners afraid of intimacy? In a perfect world, kissing booths would be found on every corner. In a not-so-perfect-but-pretty-good world, there's anonymous sex.

A few years ago I read an article about public sex recommending that men should always kiss their partners first, before engaging in any sexual act, since undercover cops won't kiss. I remember thinking what good advice this was, not because I was afraid of the cops, but because gay men don't kiss enough. Maybe that's because we use up all our public kisses at protest rallies or random acts of subversion on buses and street corners. We're here, we're queer, get used to it.

The thought of that first real kiss still makes me shake my head. It wasn't until a few months later, when another lover told me to open my mouth more, that I thought I was getting a handle on my kissing technique. I became more confident and started practising with friends at house parties. Who would have thought that I'd start playing spin the bottle in my early twenties, or that at the time I was first getting comfortable with my own sexuality, I would kiss almost as many women as men? My life became a cornucopia of kisses and it didn't matter where those kisses came from; the simple act of kissing quenched a thirst that for so long had gone unsatiated.

Around the same time I kissed Valerie Davies' knee, I remember watching my aunt make out with her race-car-driver boyfriend in the TV room while I watched *Grease*. I remember the way their heads moved in and out of the rhythm of the soundtrack during those kisses, and the urgency of their movements – which I associated with them not having a room of their own to make out in, but which I now understand as the way one feels when deep in the throes of passion. In some ways it would have been better if my first song with my first boyfriend had been something from the *Grease* soundtrack, because at that moment, sitting on the chair while my aunt and her boyfriend kissed in front of me, I knew what kind of kissing I wanted when I grew older: something that made you feel better, so much better that you didn't want to stop.

Last year I realized that I had sucked more cocks than I had kissed men, and that made me stop and think. What had I held back? What had I given away? What had been taken? Shouldn't kissing a cock count for something? Shouldn't that be considered more personal? But it isn't, really. When I look back on all the kisses that have meant something to me – the ones I've given as well as the ones I've received – blow jobs pale in comparison.

Perhaps the kisses that matter most are not the ones I have had, but the ones that never happened. I'm thinking of the time I broke up with a man I was living with, and I slept in the living room adjacent to the kitchen while he slept in the bedroom. One morning when I woke up, I could hear him through the door: the sound as he twisted the lid off the peanut butter jar, the sandpapery rasp as he spread peanut butter on his toast, the chime of the knife as he placed it in the sink. Unlike so many other mornings, when he'd come into the bedroom and kissed me on the forehead before he left for work, on this day he just left me in the living room, lying there alone with the ache of his absent kiss throbbing on my forehead. What a difference that kiss would have made. It's at moments such as these that I wish I could kiss it better myself.

SCRUPLES OPTIONAL

I t's one thing when you're not sure whether or not you should tell someone about the spinach stuck to his tooth or the drop of mustard at the side of his mouth. It's quite another when you bump into a friend at a clothing-optional beach and he has a piece of toilet paper stuck to his foreskin. "Dude, there's a piece of toilet paper on the end of your cock," doesn't sound right, even when you have the best intentions.

If the guy had a shred of spinach or a drop of mustard on his cock, I would not have a problem saying, "Dude, you have spinach on your cock," or "Dude, you have mustard on your wiener." Toilet paper – well, toilet paper changes things. Especially if it's two-ply.

Also, if it were just the two of us or a small group of friends, I could deal with the situation without making an embarrassing scene. But in larger group settings such as a crowded beach, it is far preferable to keep the attention away from someone's cock. In that context, "Dude, there's a piece of toilet paper on the end of your cock" translates into "Quick, everybody stare at the toilet paper on the end of his cock."

Why is the situation so much more delicate when the foreign object is toilet paper? What about all the other strange things you may find on bodies? Excuse me, you have a cigarette butt in your bush, a piece of gum stuck to your bum, a popsicle stick stuck to your breast, a condom wrapper between your toes. The possibilities are endless. What if someone was eating a package of M&Ms and dropped one but couldn't figure out where it went? Thank God for melts in your mouth, not in your crotch.

I'm the kind of person who usually goes ahead and wipes things off a person's face or pulls that bit of twig or whatever out of his hair. People like it when I do this. They especially like it when I save the foreign object and show them what was clinging to their body. People like to see that kind of thing. It's like going to the dentist and having a tooth extracted: you want to see what got pulled out. Maybe we like seeing the stuff that comes away from our bodies so that we can justify another person touching us.

But while I may go up to a boyfriend and pull something from his cock and show it to him without embarrassment, I would never do that to a casual acquaintance or even a good friend, and certainly not on an open beach full of people. I wish I were the kind of person who could run up to a friend and pull something from his cock and then extend my hand to show it to him. Maybe it's just as well, though – with my luck, it would probably be a piercing that would not give no matter how hard I yanked.

THE DRY HUMP BANDIT

When I was young, I knew a small black dog named Missy, who was the beloved pet of a family friend. At dinner parties, this woman drank Spanish coffees or rum and Cokes, while Missy sat on her lap as if it were a throne. Sometimes Missy hopped down on the floor to retrieve a dropped pretzel, but otherwise she just sat there all evening like a queen.

I began to babysit for that woman's children when I was a teenager, and I learned the hard way that Missy had an alter ego that was eerily like Mr Hyde. As soon as the parents closed the front door and left for the evening, Missy turned into an ass-sniffing, hump-'em-when-they're-down kind of dog. The regal Missy became the relentless Mr Dry Hump. Every leg or leg-like object in the house became a victim in waiting.

The kids had it easy. At bedtime they just closed their doors and shut out the Missy threat. I, on the other hand, had nowhere to run. On some evenings the living room felt like a battlefield. Armed with a pile of pillows and textbooks, I struggled to guard what little remained of my dignity. One false move and Missy would be on my leg. Or my arm. Or anything else she could get her paws on.

I forgot about Missy until recently, when I began a most unfortunate affair. While in bed with a certain someone, I looked up to see his eyes closed and his tongue stuck out to the side as he thrust his cock back and forth across my inner thigh with an urgency I hadn't seen since – you guessed it – Missy, the dry hump bandit. And while he kept pumping I wondered what doggy injustice I might have committed to deserve such punishment.

Had I mistreated Missy? Ignored her barking one too many times? Failed to fill her food bowl to the very top? If this is what I get for kicking a horny dog, then what will happen to me for the goldfish that died when I was four, because I filled the tank with my favourite breakfast cereal?

Sometimes karma dry humps your leg. But maybe the human dry hump bandit had nothing to do with Missy at all. Maybe he was just a lousy lay. Maybe he had won numerous Boy Scout awards for starting campfires and now had a fetish for rubbing sticks together. How else can I explain someone getting off on so much friction? Hey, buddy, ever heard of lube?

As I waited for him to finish, I fantasized looking him straight in the eye (once he opened them up again) and saying, "Wow, that was great. Now, if you could do that to the rest of my body I'd never have to exfoliate again." I am proud to say that I didn't make karmic matters worse by doing that. Instead, I let it go. Like Missy, that lousy lay will soon be forgotten – until the next one.

WHAT'S IN A NAME?

Research shows that as we grow more dependent on keyboards and cellphones, we become less comfortable writing with pen and paper. The result? Our sloppy scroll causes countless workplace accidents, accounting nightmares, and errors in the dispensing of prescriptions – not to mention an overwhelming number of snapshots left unclaimed when photo-mart staff are unable to decipher either the owner's name or the phone number. Millions and millions of dollars are spent each year rectifying such mistakes. Even more significant, one night the problem stopped me from getting laid.

How in the hell can I call someone up for a date if I can't read his name on the piece of paper he slipped me? It's not like I can phone and ask, "Is either Ron or Don there?" If I call and say, "I'm looking for man in his late twenties with dark hair who passed me this number last night," I'll sound (and be) really desperate. And I wouldn't want to just start talking to the first male voice I hear, because I could pick up his roommate or brother or father by accident. Identical twin good, other family bad. Well, usually.

If only the mystery man's teachers had worked

with him to improve his handwriting, I would have been able to call him up and get a little action. Instead, Mr What's-His-Name is running around the city passing out illegible calling cards while I stay at home choking the chicken.

Ironically, I'm not the kind of person who needs to know someone's name before I have sex with him. Tom, Dick, and Harry. Blah blah blah. Who wants to risk forgetting or mispronouncing his name – especially at the height of orgasm? The last thing I need is some post-coital man looking up at me with a glistening chest and saying, "Actually it's Tim, not Tom." Sometimes it's easier not to know. That's what makes anonymous sex anonymous. But sometimes it is practical and useful to know someone's name, such as when you want to call him on the telephone.

If a person can't write or print his name legibly, he should get help from a friend, preferably one of those girls from high school with immaculate penmanship who gathered whole sticker books full of accolades for their breathtaking technique, one of those girls who never misses out on getting laid because someone can't read her name. She could write up a whole stack of beautifully handwritten calling cards (business cards are for business, not sex). All he has to do is make sure she doesn't draw a little heart in place of the dot on any of the i's or j's. If she does, it doesn't matter whether anyone can read your name – no one will sleep with you anyway. As Leonard Cohen said, "Don't leave home with your heart on." If you ever gave your card to someone and he never called you, this could be the reason. If the someone was me, write to me c/o my publisher – and make it legible.

SNAP CRACKLE POPPERS

When I poured soy milk into my bowl of
Rice Krispies one morning not long ago,
I didn't expect any earth-shattering
epiphanies. I'll admit I was proud of having taken
the time to eat breakfast – it was one of my New
Year's resolutions – but it shouldn't be considered
a great achievement. The time may come when
eating my cereal does become a highlight, but I
hope to be in my eighties, at least, and living at
a gay nursing home that turns on the disco ball
and Gloria Gaynor's "I Will Survive" as motivation
to finish the morning meal. In the meantime, I
thought I had fifty years of uneventful breakfasts
ahead of me. I was wrong.

On that day I realized that the oh-so-innocent
sound of Rice Krispies, the snap crackle pop, the
sound that in my childhood made me pull my
cereal bowl close to my ear as if it were a sea shell
in which I could hear the sea, was really the sound
of three miniature gay men having an orgy inside
my bowl.

That's right. Snap, Crackle, and Pop were fudge-
packers! Poofs! Big 'Mos. Those geeky little
cheerleaders, or band players, or – what the hell
are they exactly? – have been having three-ways

right under my nose, all my life. The many years of speculating why Krispies would move around by themselves are over. I am vindicated. It's wasn't air bubbles like my mother told me, it was horny little men unable to control their passion. A foot here, an arm there, a head bobbing like there's no tomorrow. It's a wonder more Krispies didn't leap right up in the air.

I had to think hard before I wrote down this discovery. I don't want to "out" anybody, human or cartoon. They have careers, maybe families from before they realized they liked to be with men. What would I gain from outing a cartoon cereal spokesperson? It's not as if I would be outing Jesse Helms or some backwoods politician. And then it hit me like a slap: all these years Kellogg's has been misrepresenting the sounds emanating from our cereal bowls. It's not snap crackle pop; it's snap crackle poppers!

As a gay man, I feel it is my duty to break the chains that have been wrapped around my miniature gay brothers' desire. Poppers it will be, forever more! If you don't believe me, check it out yourself. Just don't buy a big box. Go to a small diner or a cafeteria and get one of those single-serving boxes instead. Pour on the milk and lean over the bowl – hell, get a bunch of diner patrons, the waitress, and even the cook to join you in celebration. This is not an urban myth like the story of how the letter H was banned from Alpha-Bits so children wouldn't be able to spell homosexual. It's true. Really. It is.

Up the . . . Nose?

What do you do when he asks you to cum on his face, and as you're ready to blow he tilts his head back in ecstasy and you shoot up his nose? In retrospect, I know I should have done something other than scream out laughing. Maybe I grew up reading too many of those "Laughter, the Best Medicine" columns in the *Reader's Digest*, but at the time laughter was my honest response. If only the *Reader's Digest* had a section called "Kleenex, the Best Medicine," I would have been better prepared.

I finally did offer up a box of tissues, but I wasn't quite sure of the proper etiquette for such a situation. Do I say something, or pretend that it never happened? Do I apologize, or offer to cum in his ear next time? It's not like Miss Manners has a chapter or even a paragraph devoted to the do's and don'ts of accidentally shooting up someone's nose. Then again, I'm the kind of guy who has to ask the person sitting next to me which fork to use for the salad, so even if there were a guide to sexual manners, I'd probably forget the protocols.

This wasn't the first time I've cum into an inappropriate location. There was the lover whose armpit always seemed to get in the way, the unfortunate teddy bear incident (sorry, Boo-Boo), and the time I shot onto a photograph that sat on my bedside table. (For the sake of friendship and family unity, I won't say whose photograph it was.)

But for some reason, the up-the-nose episode sticks out more than any other. It has reached pivotal sex moment status. It kept replaying inside my head for days, in the same slow-motion style that they use on news telecasts to report attempted assassinations: Kennedy, Reagan, the Pope. And just as they use those small arrows superimposed on the screen to indicate bullet entry points, my internal television had arrows pointing to his right nostril. It was as if my cock had become a gun – or at least a water pistol – and my pubes had become a grassy knoll. In the days that followed, the world seemed to revolve around that flaring nostril. Not since my first yoga class had a nostril been so significant.

I took comfort knowing that it could have been worse. There was that guy who was wanking off and just as he started to cum, his mother's cat – which, ironically, was the same kind of fluffy white cat that nudges rolls of toilet paper along the floor on those TV commercials – jumped onto his chest. That's right, he spunked the kitty, and he had to catch it and clean it up before it ran back to his mother.

Part of me still feels embarrassed about the nose incident and hopes that this kind of thing never happens again. Another part can't help but quote the old car commercial: "You asked for it, you got it." Either way, it's a sticky situation.

GAYSICLES

One of the few things I miss about my hometown is the ice cream trucks that served up a daily dose of drama to our otherwise uneventful suburban world. Many people find ice cream vendors intrusive and disruptive; I've always loved the chaos they introduce.

Within just a couple of musical notes, every kid on the block was outside waiting to buy Popsicles, or at the very least, waiting to see who bought Popsicles. So much of the gossip in my neighbourhood revolved around such moments. "Oh, there's that Nickerson kid buying another treat. Doesn't his mother worry about his teeth?"And there was many a summer night when the neighbours kept their windows open and you could hear mothers screaming, "Stay put and eat your supper! We've got frozen Kool-Aid in the freezer."

What we need in gay neighbourhoods are gay ice cream trucks, complete with rainbow Popsicles, dick-shaped sherbet, cherry-flavoured clit-on-a-stick, and licorice ice-cream chaps surrounding two buttock-shaped mounds available in either peach or mocha. There could be condoms, lube, bottled water, and strawberry-flavoured AIDS ribbons, with ten percent of each sale donated to local charities.

The drivers could be bitter drag queens, or towel boys from bathhouses. The drag queens would lament that ice cream isn't as good as it used to be. The towel boys would wear nothing but tight shorts and little flip-flops. Sometimes they would harden their nipples by rubbing cool treats on them. "Oh, it's you – sorry, I didn't recognize you without the white towel wrapped around your waist."

I can just see the logjams at apartment elevators, everyone trying to get down for a fudgsicle. And what a sight when the truck would pass a crowd of party-goers returning from the after-after-hours: they would hop and dance along to the music and buy bottled water and frozen juice bars because the drugs they took the night before had depleted all the vitamin c in their bodies. They'd tell the driver, "You're the best ice-cream driver I've ever met," just after they had told a bunch of trees they were the most beautiful trees they had ever seen. Everyone would be happy.

So the next time you walk down a quiet street on a hot day, make a mental note on how much fun it could be if a gay ice-cream truck drove by with a disco ball spinning on its roof and disco music blaring from its speakers. Sometimes all it takes is a little chaos to get neighbours talking. And if you're lucky, you'll get to share a popsicle or whatever with the cute guy from down the hall.

If I Had a Hammer

This year, having acquired a screwdriver and various other tools, I thought I was on the road to tool trauma recovery. No more late-night calls to lesbian friends when, after a whole day of trying to put together a new IKEA purchase, I'd surrender to their superior tool expertise. No more expensive repair bills; no more storage room full of broken items that I'd had to give up on. But I was wrong. Just when I thought I was on my way to butchdom, my true colours shone through.

The occasion was my new job working at a university bookstore. I was hired as a cashier to assist the regular staff during the September rush. They asked me if I wanted some extra hours moving books around the warehouse. Fine, I thought. I can carry books. I can sweat. I wore my favourite T-shirt, pants, and steel-toed army boots. I looked fabulous.

The book-moving turned out to be helping a co-worker take apart some metal shelving. I'm not talking a single IKEA bookshelf, I'm talking the big-ass shelf IKEA has in the warehouse to store all the smaller bookshelves. The co-worker, a woman with more butchness in her earlobes than I have in my entire body, told me to pick up a hammer and start whacking the shelves apart. I did so, but soon knew that I was in big trouble. When I picked up my hammer it felt and behaved like a hammer; when my co-worker picked up her hammer it became a magic wand that transformed her from an all-star women's rugby player to a ballerina performing in *Swan Lake*. But as she danced around the shelves smacking and clanging her magic wand/hammer, it occurred to me that I was the one wearing the tutu.

I told the supervisor that I would be glad to move books and that in this shelf job I would be more of a hindrance than a help, that I might even hurt myself or one of my co-workers. I'm a cashier. Cash, yes. Hammers, no.

My friend who got me the job couldn't believe that they had assigned someone like me to take down bookshelves. He went on to explain that my sissiness was M&M style – I'm hard and a little butchy on the outside, soft and sissy on the inside. He, on the other hand, was a reverse M&M, he told me. Sissy on the outside and hard inside. "That's because I'm from small-town Ontario," he said.

My friend is right: I'm a big sissy at heart. Just don't fuck with my hard candy coating. And whatever you do, don't put a hammer in my hands. There's no telling what might happen.

MY LEFT TIT

A friend of mine loves to refer to his nipples as his little red fire ants. His little red left fire ant and his little red right. He likes to describe how much they stung the night before or how they burned so bad he felt like he was engulfed in flames. The first time I heard him talk in this manner, it took me a few moments to understand what he meant. I kept thinking, "Get an exterminator, man," before I made the connection.

I love my friend's apt metaphor, but even more than that, I appreciate his special body awareness. He is the only person I ever knew who differentiates between his two nipples. It isn't good enough for him to just say "tits." He always makes a point of including "left" or "right" in his descriptions. Each tit has its own identity.

I credit my friend with helping me realize that my left tit is more sensitive than my right. Now I guide everyone over to my left side during our first night together. Sometimes I'll catch myself cooing to a new lover, "No, suck my left" whenever he pays too much attention to my right side. Why settle for less?

Over the years I have become so fixated on the joys of my left tit that I only recently realized that not everyone has a preferred side. Then I began asking friends whether they find their left tit more sensitive than their right. After the initial shock of my question wears off – it's not every day someone asks such a specific intimate question – the person usually answers me, then double-checks by giving a quick flick, pinch, squeeze, or gentle caress. Some people just give me a puzzled look and then check, using one of the aforementioned techniques. One friend started to chatter his teeth and bend his head down before he realized he couldn't reach.

Most of the guys I talked to had a preference. Only one said he'd rather have somebody play with his hair. Most of the women I asked said they didn't really care which side got the attention, though they were all quick to mention which of their breasts was larger than the other. One woman figured that she didn't need a preference since she generally squeezed her nipples together and had her partners suck on them at the same time. Another friend offered some wonderful advice: if you have an insensitive tit, don't pierce the good one. Never put all your good tits in one basket.

Whatever results you get on this poll, the fun is in the polling. I recommend asking the question in a group, preferably in a public place. One day you may find yourself, as I did, in a restaurant booth surrounded by men playing with their tits. It'll make your grilled-cheese sandwich taste better. Really.

Mr bc Leather 2000

Not long ago my mother told me that when I was six and had just received my first two-wheeler, I refused to keep it in the garage. She said I insisted on parking my bike beside my bed because the Fonz, from the TV show *Happy Days*, kept his motorcycle in his bedroom.

This shocked me for two reasons: 1) I have a good memory and could not recall anything about parking my bike beside my teddy bear-bedecked bed, and 2) I've spent so many years celebrating Wonder Woman, the Bionic Woman, and Charlie's Angels that I forgot about the Fonz, with his motorcycle, slicked-back hair, and leather jacket.

How fitting that around the time my mother reminded me about one of the few men I've ever emulated, the man who'd exclaim, "Don't touch the leather," I went to my first Mr bc Leather pageant. Those guys made the Fonz look like a big sissy. Maybe it was the gin and tonics, but I found those men to be some of the most approachable and unpretentious people I've met at a club – a breath of fresh air compared to whacked-out ravers fondling their water bottles.

To break the ice, I asked many of the West Coast leather elite whether they'd encountered a leather-scene vegetarian. They all said no, though

Seattle Leather Daddy 1998 said he'd heard about a few lesbian leather vegetarians. Then I asked Mr Seattle Leather 1999 about the difference between the Canadian leather scene and the American one. I half-expected him to say that Canadians apologize after they flog you. But he simply commented on how welcoming and supportive we all are.

In the washroom I asked a few leather guys whether they actually used the product made by the sponsor of the event, a leather cleaner, for anything other than "poppers." One guy confessed that he'd never put the stuff on his leather. Before I could ask him what he does put it on, he stepped away from the urinal, so I asked the guy who replaced him whether he'd clean his leather with the sponsor's product. He too said no, then walked away before I could ask the next question. I never did find out how they clean.

Ironically, the most pain-filled part of the event had nothing to do with the leather demonstration. During the intermission we sat through number after number of unclaimed door-prize winners. Maybe the leather guys didn't have pockets to carry their tickets. Or maybe they just wanted to give our patience a little paddle-whack.

Since the organizers never crowned a Mr Leather BC Congeniality 2000, I nominate everyone from Vancouver's leather scene. Never have I encountered so many men who excuse themselves when walking past you in a crowded room or who use their please and thank-you. Your mothers should be proud. You guys are great.

Going Bananas

Last summer, when I travelled on a Boeing 737 from Victoria to Calgary, I learned how traumatic it can be to witness a whole planeload of passengers eating bananas. The flight attendants had just passed out our lunch, consisting of a sandwich bun, a bag of potato chips (trick-or-treat sized), and a banana.

Had my trip taken place just a few days earlier, I would not have thought of touching my banana, let alone eating it, but the night before the flight, my lover at the time suggested I eat more bananas after he found out I had just had a charley horse and not an orgasm. I had not eaten a banana since the week I consumed at least twenty of them while practising oral sex techniques for my first boyfriend, so I considered the presence of the banana a sign from above. I must be meant to have frequent and painless (no charley horses) sex. Much to the dismay of my fellow passengers, I started to seat dance and hum the Chiquita Banana theme song.

I must have eaten the sandwich and the chips pretty quickly, because when the flight attendant came down the aisle with his rickety drink cart, he looked down at me with a perfectly smug expression on his face. I ordered an orange juice, then proceeded to stare down at the banana, poke it a few times, and ponder whether it came from a democratic country or one of those places run by a right-wing military regime. I then realized that it was not appropriate to question the political associations of a banana sent from the sex gods.

By the time I'd pulled back the skin and placed its head in my mouth, I experienced the banana-eater's equivalent to Spider-Man's Spider-Sense: I could feel people eating bananas around me. When I looked up I saw grandmas and grandpas, businessmen, women in red jumpsuits, unaccompanied minors, and entire families all going down on bananas. It was as though I had been cast as an extra for a *Twilight Zone* episode guest-directed by Sigmund Freud. Needless to say, I went cuckoo.

Had the drinks cart not been in the way, I might have run down the aisle and pulled at one of the emergency exit doors to provoke a depressurization. Everyone knows you can't eat a banana with an oxygen mask on. Instead, I just sat there as everyone tried to avoid each other's eyes. The people in the aisle seats pretended to be interested in the floor-level lighting that comes on during takeoffs and landings. The centre-seaters alternated between staring down at their in-flight magazines and rearranging the empty chip bags and plastic wrappers in the wicker baskets that lunch had come in. The people in the window seats tried to hide from the banana incident by pretending to recognize their houses or other landmarks from above.

And the flight attendants? The flight attendants just walked the aisles with perfectly smug looks on their faces.

COME PREPARED

When I told a group of friends that I intended to write about cum towels, one of them asked me what I meant. To say that his question surprised me would be more than an understatement. How could there be a man alive who did not understand the term?

"Cum towels," I said. "You know, cum towels."

Finally I had to explain. I said that sometimes it's not really a towel, but anything within arm's reach of your bed. T-shirts, jogging pants, pillow cases, socks, that roll of toilet paper you keep on the nightstand for your "perpetual runny nose."

That's why when you go over to someone's place, you should always obey cum towel rule number two: never touch anything within three feet of his bed. Ten feet if he plays basketball. (Cum towel rule number one, of course, being never use your teddy bear.)

By this time my friend knew what I meant, and we all started to share cum towel stories. My boyfriend told about the time he got up late for his biomedical ethics class and grabbed the first shirt he saw – his favourite shirt, the bright orange one with a picture of Harmony smurf blowing a trumpet on the front. Everything seemed fine until halfway through the class, when he realized that his shirt was a little bit crunchier than usual. He spent the rest of the hour pondering the ethical thing to do in that situation.

Another friend said that when he was younger he had owned a hamster – not a gerbil, he insisted, but a hamster – named Muppy, which kept getting him into trouble because he used the good family bath towels when he cleaned the cage. His mother ended up making a special towel with the word *Muppy* embroidered on it so she could keep it separate from all the human laundry. Muppy may no longer be with us, but his towel has continued to serve an almost sacred purpose in the bedroom.

I told everyone about the time I met this guy in Seattle, at the apartment he had just moved into. We ended up having sex on the floor in/on his sleeping bag, but when I got up to get a towel, I found out that he hadn't unpacked them yet. Or the toilet paper. Or the face cloths. Or the paper towels in the kitchen. Nothing.

And since I had only brought the clothes on my back and he hadn't moved his in yet, I ended up using my socks. Which would not have been a big problem had I intended to go straight home in the morning. But I didn't, so there was only one thing to do. I spent a good part of the next day walking around Seattle being careful not to lift my legs too far off the ground for fear that my exposed ankles would show and everyone would mistake me for Don Johnson, back in his *Miami Vice* days.

GAYLAND

When I heard that Playland, the trashy amusement park in Vancouver, had declared a special Gay Day during Pride Week, I wanted to go right away. But when we arrived at the entrance gates, I was a bit disappointed. I had expected more fanfare – at least a giant banner welcoming the queer masses. Maybe I've attended too many Pride parades, but I expected to see the Dykes on Bikes driving around the various roller coasters and carnival games, some of them with their prize-winning stuffed animals propped on the handlebars of their Harleys.

At the ticket window, we were asked by an older woman whether or not we were there for Pride. How did that poor woman feel about spending the whole day asking complete strangers whether they were gay or straight or somewhere in between? I hoped that she'd had some previous contact with the gay community, some moment that had rubbed a little bit of gaydar onto her. She wore the same look as someone who is trying to figure out whether a tourist is from England or Australia.

Only later did I find out why the woman had to ask the all-important Pride question: anyone who went in without identifying him or herself as a "Pride participant" had to pay an extra three dollars. Rumour has it that a friend of ours screamed out to those standing in the "not proud" ticket lineup, pointing out that if they joined the Pride lineup and said they were gay, they would save three dollars. (Does that mean you save a dollar fifty if you're bisexual?)

Nobody switched lines, which surprised me – I would certainly say I'm straight for three dollars. But then again, I'm the sort of person who will pick up an empty can for the five-cent deposit. Three bucks, that's sixty cans.

The other highlights of the day included winning a horse derby box game against a bunch of fourteen-year-old girls and riding the Spider at the same time as the cute guy at the Body Shop who sells me loofah. I didn't see any drag queens on the roller coasters, though I did have an ominous premonition of a drag queen screaming that she lost her wig and nobody noticing – everyone screams on roller coasters – and the car behind her derailing on her synthetic bob. Fortunately that never happened. For my daily dose of drama I watched a leather daddy navigate his handlebar moustache around a great big cotton candy.

If I could change anything about Gay Day at Playland it would be my unpleasant encounter with a woman wearing poorly applied lipstick who passed us a religious pamphlet declaring that we were all sinners. Maybe Playland will host a Bigots Day, and I can walk up behind her and get three dollars off the price of admission for saying I'm a bigot. Ahhh, the sweet taste of revenge.

THE COCK IN COCKTAIL

One spring evening in Victoria, when I performed a piece of writing about seeing my first female stripper, a woman friend in the crowd told the story of a male stripper who stuck his cock in her friend's cocktail. I'd never heard of a stripper doing such a thing. Sure, I knew about Dan, the stripper at the Dufferin Hotel who used to bring chickens onstage with him (dead and store-bought), and I've seen a lifetime's worth of strippers who "accidentally" slap their meat against the faces of unsuspecting onlookers. I've even seen a female stripper take a McDonald's chocolate chip cookie from some guy in the front row, rub it against her pussy, and give it back to him. (To my horror, he ate it.)

Perhaps many strippers have stuck their cocks into cocktails, but I had yet to encounter one. This made me feel like a youngster again, for I'd learned something new, thus disproving the old adage that you can't teach an old dirty dog new tricks.

My friend went on to express her shock that the woman had kept on sipping her drink as if nothing had happened. Everyone at my table, including myself, agreed that a cock in your cocktail was gross and that we wouldn't have kept drinking.

After a few moments, however, I had second thoughts. What would be more obscene: wasting an otherwise perfectly good drink, or drinking a drink with a twist of dink? If I'd stick that cock inside my mouth, why wouldn't I want it in my cocktail?

So I said to my friends, "But would you stick that cock in your mouth?" This was followed by the kind of silence that often settles on a crowd at tragic or poignant moments, such as when your favourite figure skater falls on the ice and you realize his Olympic dream has ended. Then everyone, including the straight boy, nodded their heads in agreement. We were hypocritical cocksuckers.

After that I couldn't stop thinking about when I would and wouldn't want people's naked bodies to come in contact with my meals. What if there were nudist buffets, stripper day at the local pancake shop – when he sits on your pancakes he always leaves a good impression – and bartenders who use their cocks to draw the shamrock on the foam of your Guinness? During the ferry ride home I daydreamed about the staff of the Pacific Buffet on the upper deck of the ship, imagining them working in the buff, so that rough seas might cause a flapping cock or off-balanced buttock to graze the potato salad or the clam chowder. Thank God this never happened in real life. It's one thing to have a cock in your cocktail and quite another to have an ass in your salad.

THE MOANER SIXTY-NINER

The attendant asked me to sign an insurance waiver and a small slip of paper with the number 108 printed on the corner. When I passed the signed papers back under the Plexiglas partition, a buzzer sounded, and by instinct I pulled open the door in front of me. Just inside the door a man with a white towel wrapped around his waist stood at the pay phone, cradling the receiver between his jaw and his shoulder, dialing a number with one hand and tracing circles on his chest with the other. I thought back to all the times men had finger-written words on my back and asked me to guess what they were. I stared at the man's hand stroking his chest. It didn't look like he was spelling anything.

The attendant took my sixteen dollars, then handed me a small white towel and a velcro wristband with two keys attached. When I realized he would not be giving me anything else, I walked in, past a TV room filled with more men in white towels, more white towels with men.

The bathhouse reminded me of a hotel, only with much narrower hallways and smaller rooms. Each time I walked past a room with the door left open, I was surprised to find it occupied by a naked man rather than a maid with a cleaning cart. I located my room and held my wristband hand close enough to the doorknob so that I could turn the key with my other hand. It did not occur to me just to take off my wristband, unlock the door, then put the wristband back on.

The room contained a bed that reminded me of a doctor's examining table, and a tan-coloured locker that reminded me of high school. I opened the locker and this time I undid my wristband first. I took off my coat, my shoes and socks, my black turtleneck, my jeans and underwear, and placed them inside the locker. It felt strange not to have to hang my shoes on a hook by the laces, strange that I could slide them right onto the locker floor without having to compete with binders and textbooks.

I sat down on my bed and listened to the noises emanating from the rooms around me. It was as if every ghost I'd ever heard on *Scooby-Doo* and all the zombies, witches, monsters, and headless horsemen that haunted my childhood Saturday mornings, had rented rooms in this very bathhouse. For some reason I thought of the Miner Forty-Niner, the bearded gold prospector ghost who haunted an abandoned mineshaft with his pickaxe and moans. What if he came here and paid sixteen bucks for a wristband and a white towel? Would the other ghosts refer to him as the Moaner Sixty-Niner? Did he feel, on nights like this, as though he had found the gold that he'd been looking for all those years? Life has so many mysteries. I closed my door, walked out into the hallway, and went in search of a gold rush of my own.

photo: Brad Cran

BILLEH NICKERSON
was born on Valentine's
Day, 1972, in Halifax,
Nova Scotia. He grew
up in Langley, B.C,. and
now lives in Vancouver
where he is editor of
PRISM international and
a contributing editor to
Geist magazine. He is
author of the poetry book
The Asthmatic Glassblower,
nominated for the
Publishing Triangle Gay
Men's Poetry Prize, and is
co-editing an anthology
called *Skank: A Book of
Questionable Tastes*, to
be published by Arsenal
Pulp in 2004.

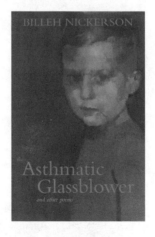